A-Z BRACKNELL

CONTENT[S]

Inde[x]
Villag[e]
selec[t]

G000126050

REFERENC[E]

Motorway	**M4**
A Road	A330
Proposed	
B Road	B3034
Dual Carriageway	
One-way Street	
Traffic flow on A Roads is also indicated by a heavy line on the driver's left.	
Restricted Access	
Pedestrianized Road	
Track / Footpath	
Residential Walkway	
Railway	Station / Level Crossing
Built-up Area	BENSON RD.
Local Authority Boundary	
Posttown Boundary	
Postcode Boundary (within Posttown)	
Map Continuation	12
Car Park (Selected)	P

Churc[h]	
Cycleway (Selected)	
Fire Station	■
Hospital	(H)
House Numbers (A & B Roads only)	15 3
Information Centre	𝒊
National Grid Reference	480
Police Station	▲
Post Office	★
Toilet:	
without facilities for the Disabled	▽
with facilities for the Disabled	▽
Disabled facilities only	▽
Educational Establishment	
Hospital or Hospice	
Industrial Building	
Leisure or Recreational Facility	
Place of Interest	
Public Building	
Shopping Centre or Market	
Other Selected Buildings	

SCALE: 1:15,840 4 inches (10.16 cm) to 1 mile, 6.31 cm to 1 kilometre

0	¼	½	¾	1 Mile

0	250	500	750	1 Kilometre

Copyright of Geographers' A-Z Map Company Limited

Fairfield Road, Borough Green, Sevenoaks, Kent TN15 8PP
Telephone: 01732 781000 (Enquiries & Trade Sales)
        01732 783422 (Retail Sales)

www.a-zmaps.co.uk

Copyright © Geographers' A-Z Map Co. Ltd.

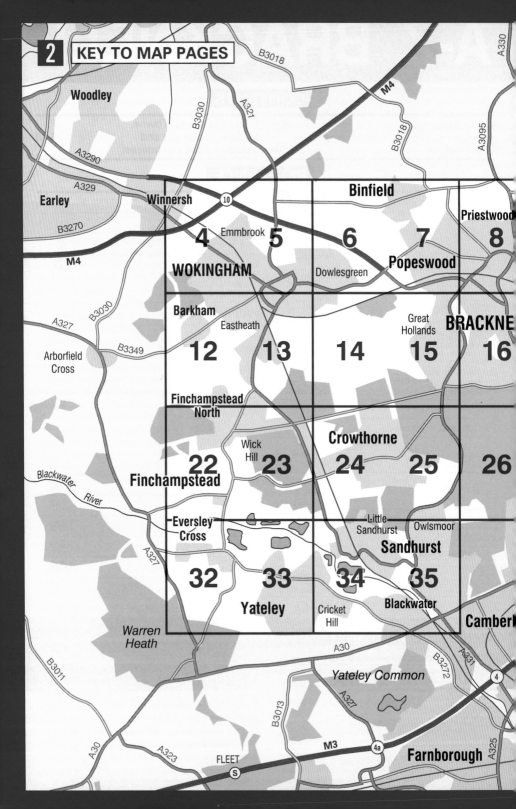

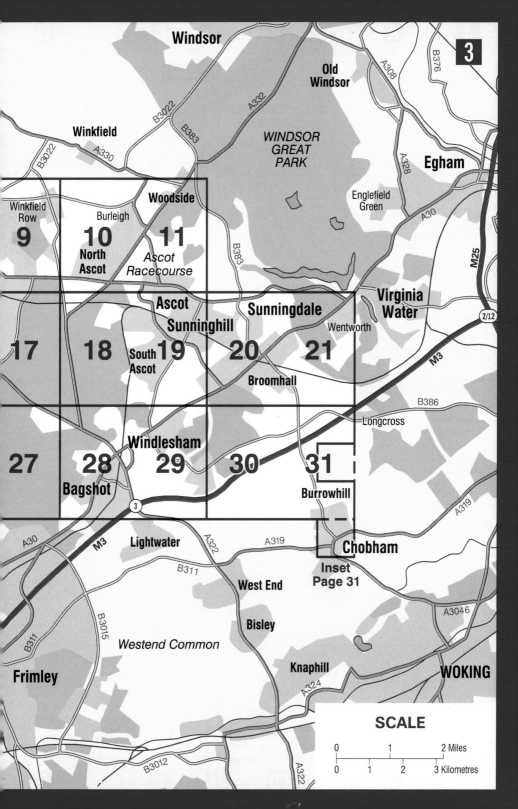

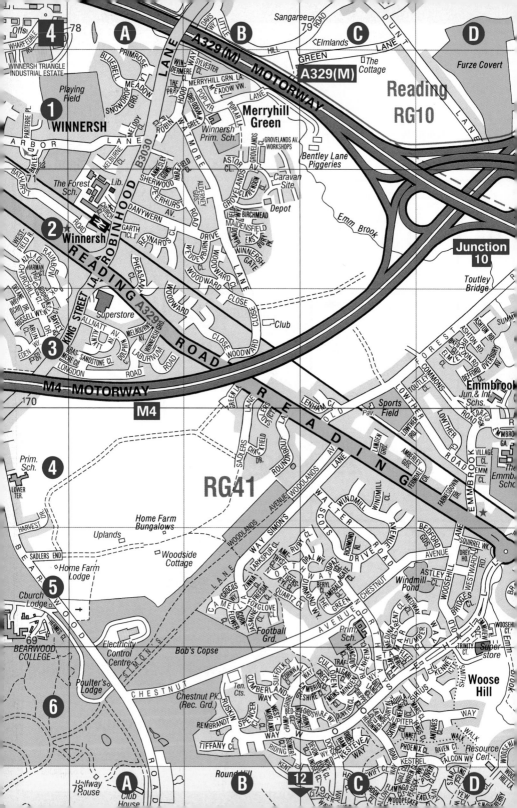

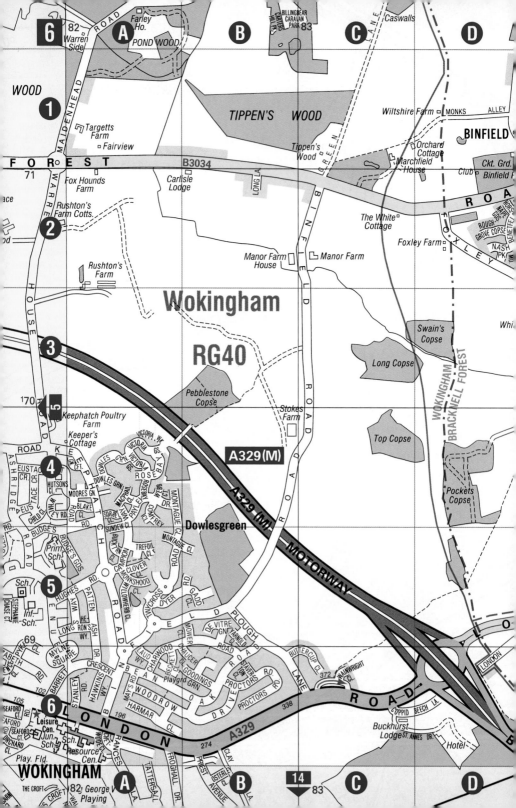

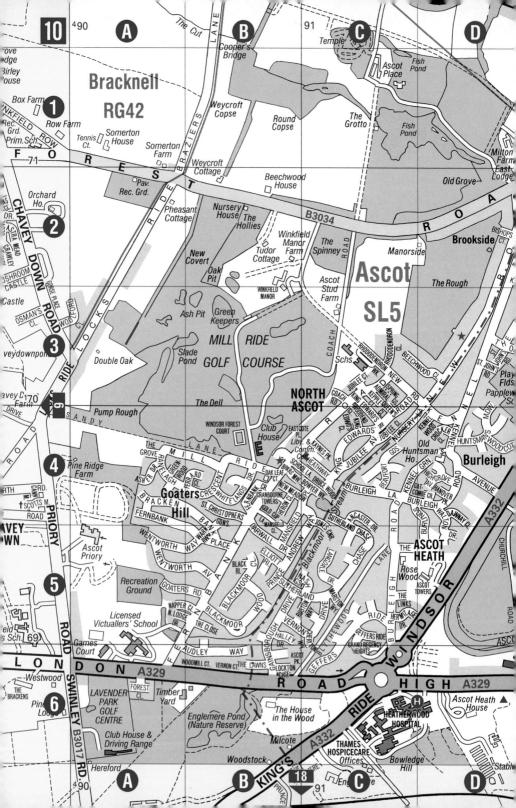

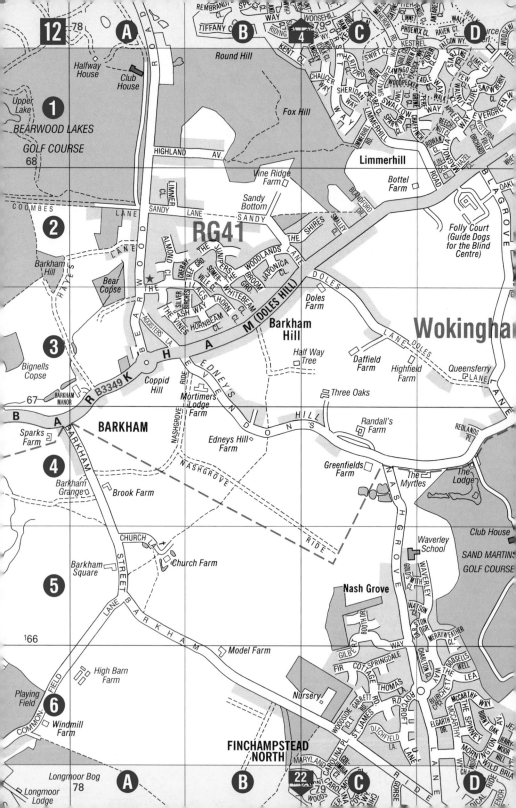

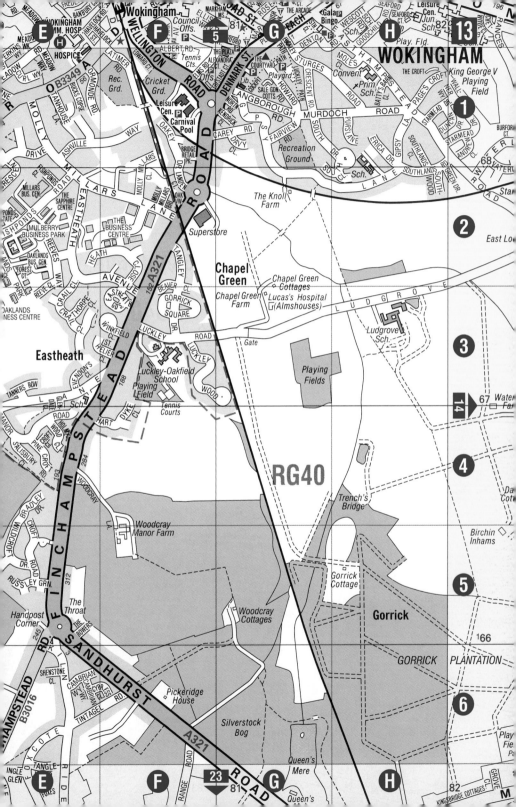

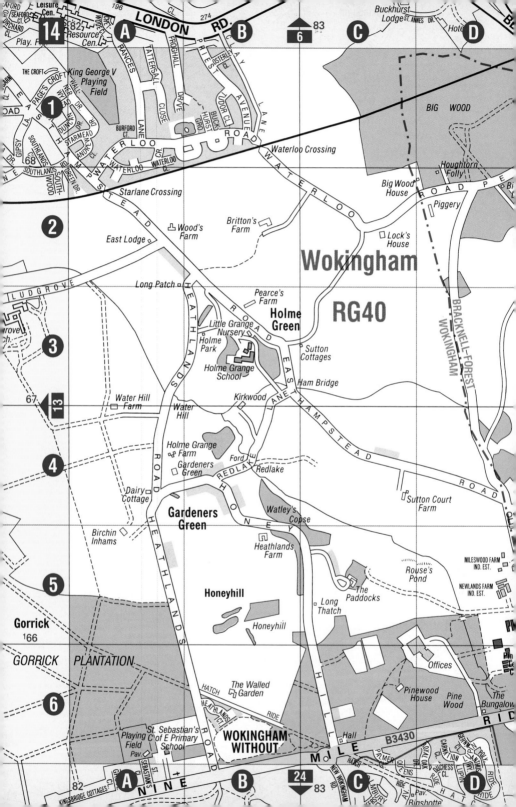

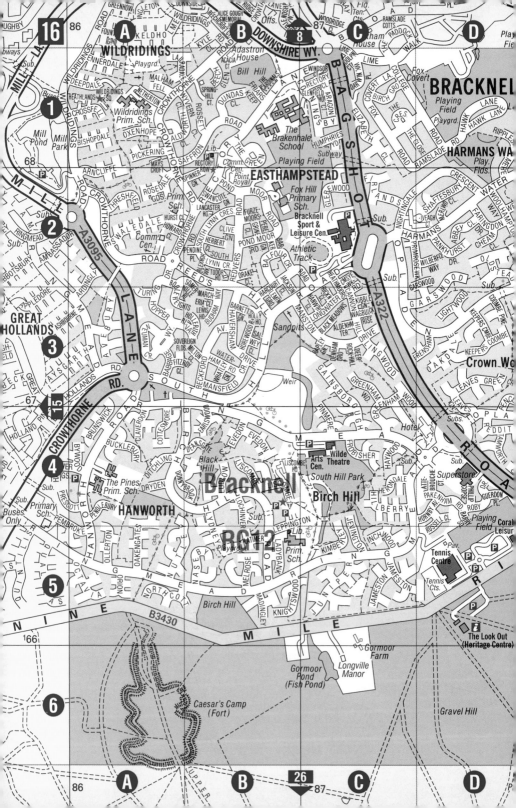

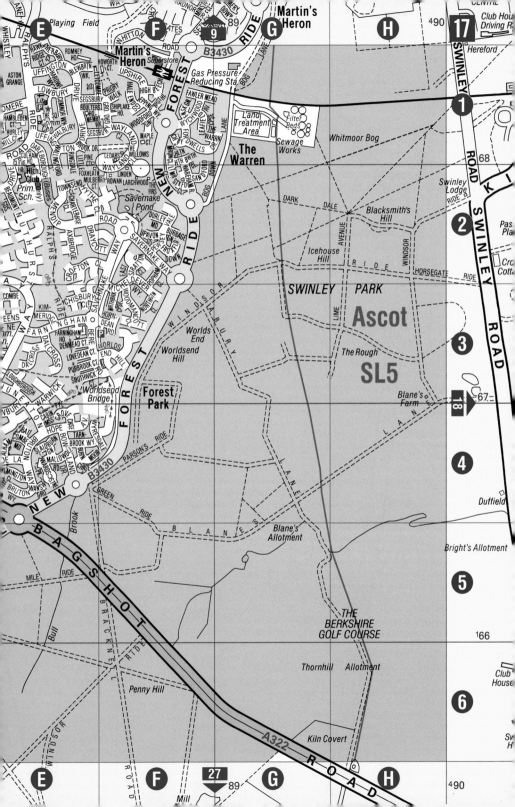

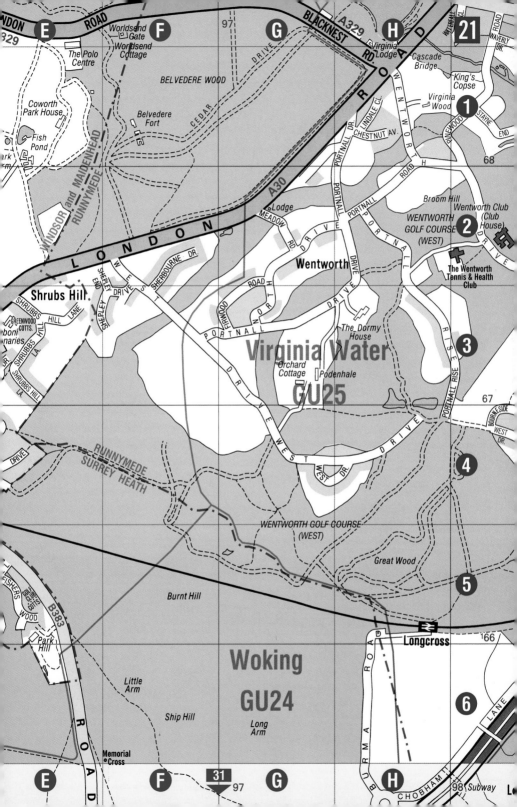

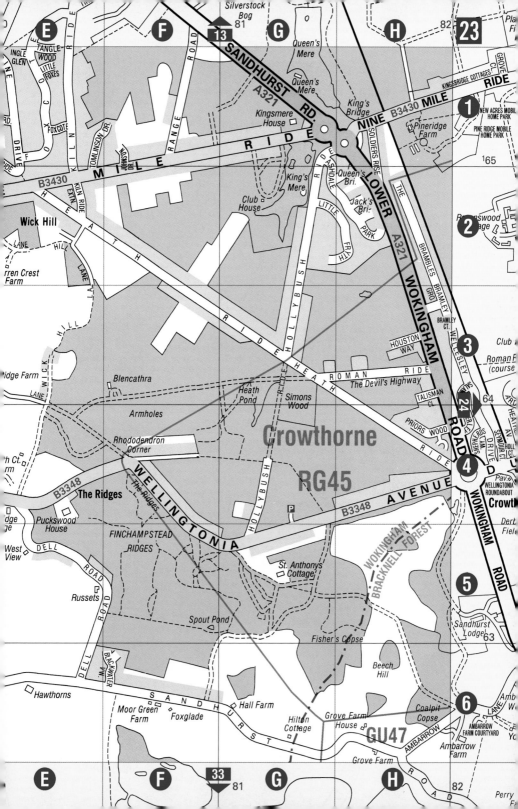

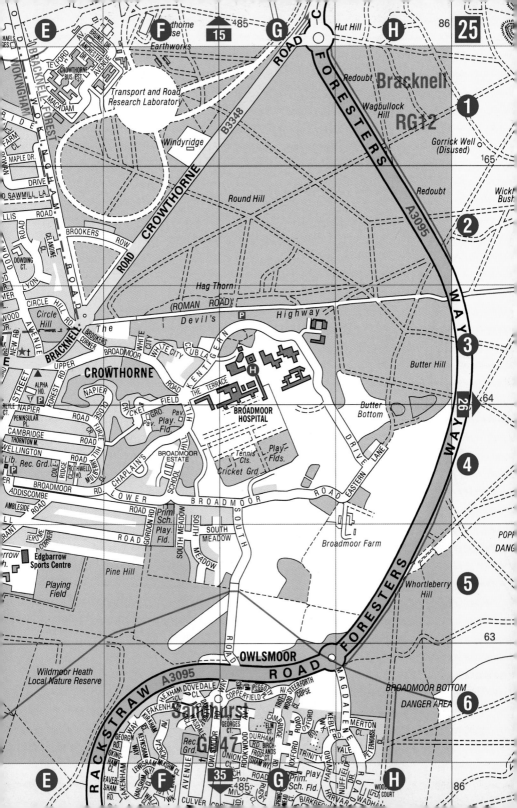

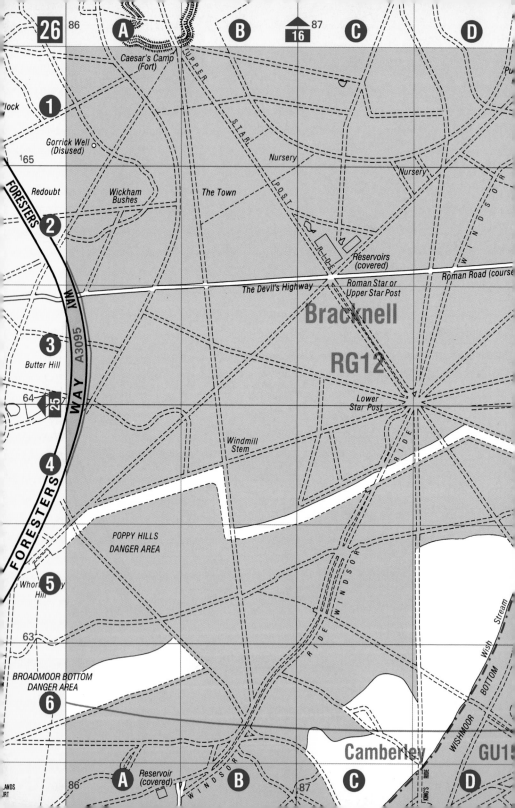

Caesar's Camp
(Fort)

1

lock

Gorrick Well
(Disused)

165

Redoubt

FORESTERS

2

Wickham
Bushes

The Town

Nursery

Nursery

Reservoirs
(covered)

The Devil's Highway

Roman Road (course

Roman Star or
Upper Star Post

Bracknell

WAY

A3095

3

Butter Hill

RG12

64

25

Lower
Star Post

4

FORESTERS

Windmill
Stem

RIDE

WINDSOR

POPPY HILLS
DANGER AREA

5

Whort-ly
Hill

63

RIDE WINDSOR

Wish Stream

BROADMOOR BOTTOM
DANGER AREA

WISHMOOR BOTTOM

6

Camberley

GU19

ANDS
RT

86

A

Reservoir
(covered)

B

WINDSOR

87

C

D

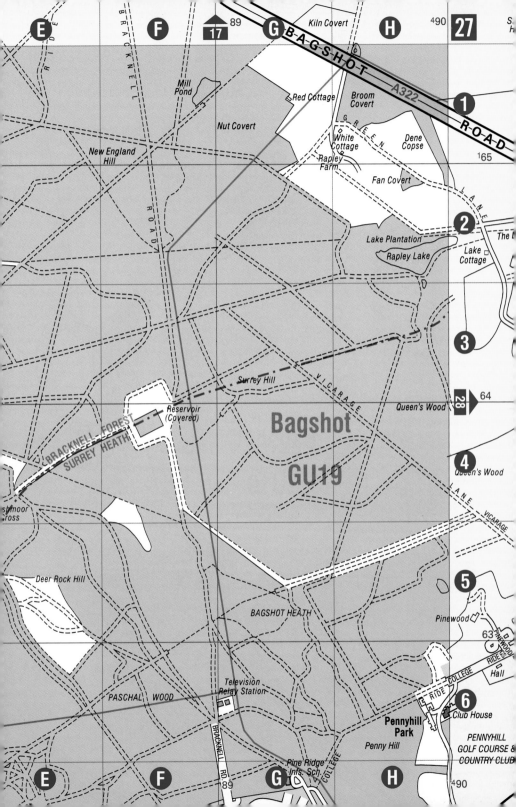

E   **F**   ▲ 89 17   **G** BAGSHOT   A322   **H** 490   27

Kiln Covert

ROAD

165

1

Red Cottage   Broom Covert

Mill Pond

Nut Covert

White Cottage   Dene Copse

New England Hill

Rapley Farm

Fan Covert

R O A D

Lake Plantation

Rapley Lake

Lake Cottage

2

The L

3

Surrey Hill

VICARAGE

Queen's Wood

28 64

Reservoir (Covered)

BRACKNELL FOREST

SURREY HEATH

Bagshot

GU19

Queen's Wood

4

shmoor ross

LANE

VICARAGE

Deer Rock Hill

5

Pinewood

63

Television Relay Station

PASCHAL WOOD

BAGSHOT HEATH

COLLEGE

RIDE 62

Hall

RIDE

6

Club House

BRACKNELL RD

Pennyhill Park

Penny Hill

PENNYHILL GOLF COURSE & COUNTRY CLUB

Pine Ridge Infs. Sch.

COLLEGE

E   **F** 89   **G**   **H** 490

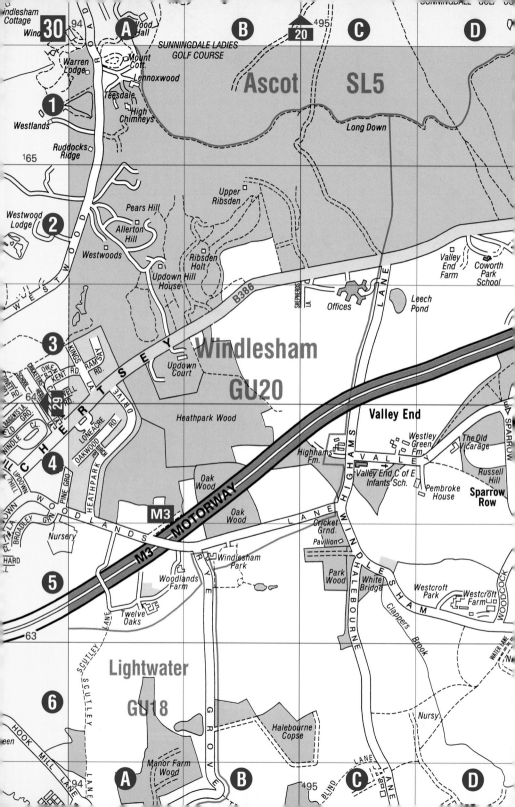

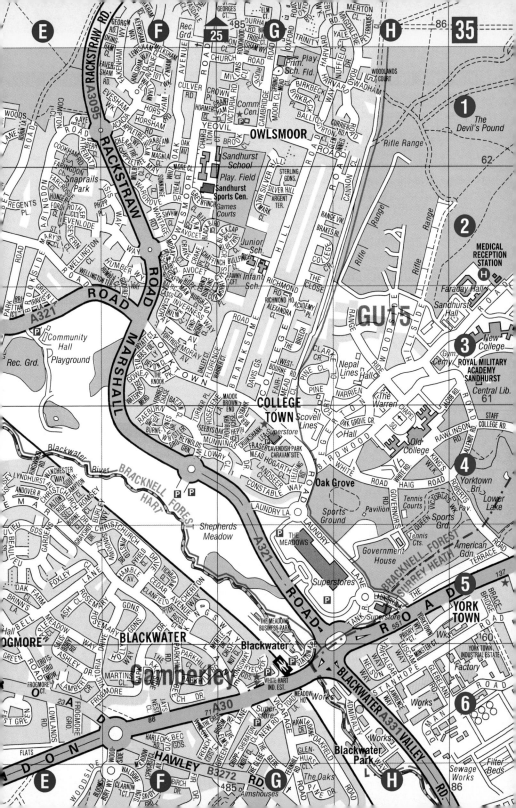

INDEX

Including Streets, Places & Areas, Hospitals & Hospices, Industrial Estates,
Selected Flats & Walkways, Stations and Selected Places of Interest.

HOW TO USE THIS INDEX

1. Each street name is followed by its Postcode District and then by its Locality abbreviation(s) and then by its map reference;
e.g. **Abingdon Rd.** GU47: Sand . . . .2E **35** is in the GU47 Postcode District and the Sandhurst Locality and is to be found in square 2E on page **35**. The page number is shown in bold type.

2. A strict alphabetical order is followed in which Av., Rd., St., etc. (though abbreviated) are read in full and as part of the street name;
e.g. **Allsmoor La.** appears after **All Saints Ri.** but before **All Souls Rd.**

3. Streets and a selection of flats and walkways too small to be shown on the maps, appear in the index with the thoroughfare to which it is connected shown in brackets; e.g. **Boveney Ho.** RG12: Brac . . . .1E **17** *(off Segsbury Gro.)*

4. Addresses that are in more than one part are referred to as not continuous.

5. Places and areas are shown in the index in **BLUE TYPE** and the map reference is to the actual map square in which the town centre or area is located and not to the place name shown on the map; e.g. **ASCOT** 1E **19**

6. An example of a selected place of interest is Novello Theatre 2H **19**

7. An example of a station is Ascot Station (Rail) 1E **19**

8. An example of a hospital or hospice is BROADMOOR HOSPITAL 3G **25**

GENERAL ABBREVIATIONS

All. : Alley	**Dr.** : Drive	**Info.** : Information	**Rd.** : Road
App. : Approach	**E.** : East	**La.** : Lane	**Rdbt.** : Roundabout
Av. : Avenue	**Ent.** : Enterprise	**Lit.** : Little	**Sth.** : South
Bri. : Bridge	**Est.** : Estate	**Lwr.** : Lower	**Sq.** : Square
Bus. : Business	**Fld.** : Field	**Mnr.** : Manor	**St.** : Street
Cvn. : Caravan	**Flds.** : Fields	**Mans.** : Mansions	**Ter.** : Terrace
Cen. : Centre	**Gdns.** : Gardens	**Mdw.** : Meadow	**Up.** : Upper
Circ. : Circle	**Gth.** : Garth	**Mdws.** : Meadows	**Va.** : Vale
Cl. : Close	**Ga.** : Gate	**M.** : Mews	**Vw.** : View
Comn. : Common	**Gt.** : Great	**Mt.** : Mount	**Wlk.** : Walk
Cnr. : Corner	**Grn.** : Green	**Nth.** : North	**W.** : West
Cotts. : Cottages	**Gro.** : Grove	**Pde.** : Parade	**Yd.** : Yard
Ct. : Court	**Hgts.** : Heights	**Pk.** : Park	
Cres. : Crescent	**Ho.** : House	**Pl.** : Place	
Cft. : Croft	**Ind.** : Industrial	**Ri.** : Rise	

LOCALITY ABBREVIATIONS

Asc : **Ascot**	Coll T : **College Town**	Owl : **Owlsmoor**	Wink : **Winkfield**
Bag : **Bagshot**	Crow : **Crowthorne**	Sand : **Sandhurst**	Wink R : **Winkfield Row**
Bark : **Barkham**	Ever : **Eversley**	Sind : **Sindlesham**	Winn : **Winnersh**
Binf : **Binfield**	Finch : **Finchampstead**	S'dale : **Sunningdale**	Woki : **Wokingham**
Blac : **Blackwater**	Haw : **Hawley**	S'hill : **Sunninghill**	Yate : **Yateley**
Brac : **Bracknell**	Hurst : **Hurst**	Vir W : **Virginia Water**	
Camb : **Camberley**	Ligh : **Lightwater**	Warf : **Warfield**	
Chob : **Chobham**	Long : **Longcross**	Wind : **Windlesham**	

A

Abbey Cl. RG12: Brac 2D **16**
RG40: Woki 5G **5**
Abbey Pl. RG42: Warf 1C **8**
Abbeywood SL5: S'dale . . .4C **20**
Abbotsbury RG12: Brac 2H **15**
Abingdon Cl. RG12: Brac . . .2E **17**
Abingdon Rd. GU47: Sand . . .2E **35**
Abury La. RG12: Brac 3G **17**
Acacia Av. GU47: Owl 1F **35**
Acacia Ct. RG12: Brac 1B **16**
Academy Pl. GU47: Coll T . . .3G **35**
Acer Cl. RG42: Warf 4G **9**
Ackrells Mead
GU47: Sand 1B **34**
Acorn Dr. RG40: Woki 5G **5**
Acorn Rd. GU17: Blac 5D **34**
Addiscombe Rd.
RG45: Crow 4E **25**
Admiral Kepple Ct.
SL5: Asc 3C **10**
Admiralty Way
GU15: Camb 6H **35**
Agar Cres. RG42: Brac 3B **8**
Agate Cl. RG41: Woki 5C **4**
Aggisters La. RG41: Woki . . .3A **12**
Agincourt SL5: Asc 6G **11**

Agincourt Cl. RG41: Woki 6C **4**
Alben Rd. RG42: Binf 1E **7**
Albert Rd. GU19: Bag 6C **28**
RG40: Woki 1F **13**
RG42: Brac 4B **8**
RG45: Crow 3D **24**
Albert Wlk. RG45: Crow 3D **24**
Albion Rd. GU47: Sand 3D **34**
Albury Cl. KT16: Long 1H **31**
Alcot Cl. RG45: Crow 4D **24**
Aldenham Ter.
RG12: Brac 3C **16**
Alderbrook Cl.
RG45: Crow 4A **24**
Alder Gro. GU46: Yate 5G **33**
Alderman Willey Cl.
RG41: Woki 6F **5**
Alderney Gdns.
RG41: Winn 2B **4**
Aldridge Pk. RG42: Wink R . .2H **9**
Aldworth Cl. RG12: Brac 1A **16**
Aldworth Gdns.
RG45: Crow 3C **24**
Alexander Wlk.
RG12: Brac 2B **16**
Alexandra Cl.
GU47: Coll T 3G **35**
Alexandra Ct. RG40: Woki . . .1G **13**
Alford Cl. GU47: Sand 3C **34**

Alice Gough Homes
RG12: Brac 6B **8**
Allenby Rd. GU15: Camb 4H **35**
Allendale Cl. GU47: Sand . . .6C **24**
Allnatt Av. RG41: Winn 3A **4**
All Saints Cl. RG40: Woki . . .5G **5**
All Saints Ri. RG42: Warf 3D **8**
Allsmoor La. RG12: Brac 6F **9**
All Souls Rd. SL5: Asc 1E **19**
Almond Cl. RG41: Woki 2A **12**
Alpha Ho. RG45: Crow 3E **25**
Alpha Rd. GU24: Chob 3H **31**
Alpine Cl. SL5: S'hill 3H **19**
Alton Ride GU17: Blac 4E **35**
Ambarrow Cres.
GU47: Sand 1B **34**
Ambarrow Farm Courtyard
GU47: Sand 6A **24**
Ambarrow La.
GU47: Sand 6H **23**
Ambassador RG12: Brac 2H **15**
Ambassador, The
SL5: S'dale 4D **20**
Amberley Gdns.
RG41: Woki 4C **4**
Ambleside RG45: Crow 4E **25**
AMEN CORNER 6F **7**
Amen Cnr. Bus. Pk.
RG12: Brac 6F **7**

Amethyst Cl. RG41: Woki 5B **4**
Ancaster Dr. SL5: Asc 4C **10**
Anders Cnr. RG42: Brac 4H **7**
Anderson Pl. GU19: Bag 4C **28**
Andover Rd. GU17: Blac 4E **35**
Andrew Cl. RG40: Woki 1A **14**
Angel Pl. RG42: Binf 2E **7**
Anneforde Pl. RG42: Brac . . .3A **8**
Annesley Gdns.
RG41: Winn 2A **4**
Antares Cl. RG41: Woki 6D **4**
Anthony Wall RG42: Warf 4F **9**
Apple Cl. RG41: Woki 1D **12**
Appledore RG12: Brac 3H **15**
Appledore Pl. RG42: Brac . . .4A **8**
Appletree Way
GU47: Owl 1F **35**
Apsey Cl. RG42: Binf 3G **7**
Aquila Cl. RG41: Woki 6C **4**
Aragon Cl. RG12: Brac 1C **16**
Aragon Rd. GU46: Yate 6G **33**
Arbor La. RG41: Winn 1A **4**
Arcade, The RG40: Woki 6G **5**
Arden Cl. RG12: Brac 5F **9**
Ardingly RG12: Brac 3A **16**
Ardwell Cl. RG45: Crow 3A **24**
Arenal Dr. RG45: Crow 5D **24**
Argent Ter. GU47: Coll T 2G **35**
Arkwright Dr. RG42: Brac 5F **7**

Arlington Bus. Pk.—Brickfields Ind. Pk.

Arlington Bus. Pk.
RG12: Brac 5A 8
Arlington Cl. RG42: Brac 4A 8
Arlington Sq. RG12: Brac 5A 8
Arlott Cl. RG27: Ever 2C 32
Armitage Ct. SL5: S'hill 3G 19
Armoury La. RG45: Crow 5C 24
Arncliffe RG12: Brac 2A 16
Arnett Av. RG40: Finch 1C 22
Arthur Rd. RG41: Woki 6E 5
Arthurstone Birches
RG42: Binf 1F 7
Arun Cl. RG41: Winn 3A 4
ASCOT 1E 19
ASCOT HEATH 5D 10
Ascot Pk. SL5: Asc 6B 10
Ascot Racecourse 5D 10
Ascot Station (Rail) 1E 19
Ascot Towers SL5: Asc 5D 10
Ashbourne RG12: Brac 3H 15
Ash Cl. GU17: Blac 5E 35
Ash Ct. RG40: Woki 6G 5
Ashdale Pk. RG40: Finch 2G 23
Ashdown Cl. RG12: Brac 5G 9
Asher Dr. SL5: Asc 4A 10
Ashfield Grn. GU46: Yate 5B 34
Ashley Dr. GU17: Blac 6E 35
Ashridge Grn. RG42: Brac 4B 8
Ashridge Rd. RG40: Woki 4H 5
Ashton Rd. RG41: Woki 3D 4
Ashurst Pk. SL5: S'hill 6H 11
Ashville Way RG41: Woki 1E 13
Ash Way RG41: Woki 3A 12
Ashwood Pl. SL5: S'dale 4A 20
Aspin Way GU17: Blac 5D 34
Astley Cl. RG41: Woki 5D 4
Aston Grange RG12: Brac 1E 17
Astor Cl. RG41: Winn 1B 4
Astra Mead RG42: Wink R 2H 9
Atfield Gro. GU20: Wind 4H 29
Atrebatti Rd. GU47: Sand 1E 35
Atrium Ct. RG12: Brac 5C 8
Attebrouche Ct.
RG12: Brac 4D 16
Atte La. RG42: Warf 2C 8
Audley Way SL5: Asc 6B 10
Augustine Wlk. RG42: Warf ...3E 9
Avebury RG12: Brac 3A 16
Avenue, The GU18: Ligh 6E 29
GU24: Chob 6H 31
RG40: Woki 5G 15
RG45: Crow 2C 24
SL5: Asc 3D 10
Avery Cl. RG40: Finch 2D 22
Avocet Cres. GU47: Coll T ...2F 35
Avon Ct. RG42: Binf 2E 7
Avon Gro. RG12: Brac 3C 8
Axbridge RG12: Brac 2E 17
Aylesham Way GU46: Yate ...4F 33
Aysgarth RG12: Brac 3H 15
Azalea Cl. RG41: Winn 2A 4

B

Babbage Way RG12: Brac ...3A 16
Back Dr. RG45: Crow 5D 24
Back of High St.
GU24: Chob 4G 31
Bacon Cl. GU47: Coll T 3F 35
Badgers Holt GU46: Yate 5F 33
Badgers Sett RG45: Crow 3B 24
Badgers Way RG12: Brac 4F 9
BAGSHOT 5C 28
Bagshot Grn. GU19: Bag 6C 28
Bagshot Rd. GU19: Bag 5E 17
GU24: Chob 4G 31
RG12: Bag, Brac 6B 8
SL5: Asc 6F 19
Bagshot Station (Rail) 4C 28
Baigents La. GU20: Wind 4H 29
Baileys Cl. GU17: Blac 6E 35
Balfour Cres. RG12: Brac 2B 16
Balintore Ct. GU47: Coll T ...2F 35
Ballencrieff Rd.
SL5: S'dale 4B 20
Balliol Way GU47: Owl 1G 35
Banbury RG12: Brac 4E 17
Banbury Cl. RG41: Woki 6E 5
Bankside RG40: Finch 2D 22
Bannister Gdns.
GU46: Yate 5B 34
RG27: Ever 2C 32
Bardeen Pl. RG12: Brac 6D 8
Barker Grn. RG12: Brac 2B 16
Barkers Mdw. SL5: Asc 4B 10
BARKHAM 4A 12
BARKHAM HILL 2A 12
Barkham Mnr. RG41: Bark ...3A 12
Barkham Ride
RG40: Finch 5A 12
Barkham St. RG40: Bark 4A 12
Barkhart Dr. RG40: Woki 5G 5
Barkhart Gdns. RG40: Woki ...5G 5
Barkis Mead GU47: Owl 6G 25
Barley Gdns. RG41: Winn 1A 4
Barley Mead RG42: Warf 3E 9
Barn Cl. RG12: Brac 5D 8
Barnett Ct. RG12: Brac 5D 8
Barnett Grn. RG12: Brac 3B 16
Barn Fld. GU46: Yate 5H 33
Barnmead GU24: Chob 3H 31
Barracane Dr. RG45: Crow ...3C 24
Barrett Cres. RG40: Woki 6H 5
Barry Sq. RG12: Brac 4D 16
Bartholomew Pl.
RG42: Warf 3E 9
Bartons Dr. GU46: Yate 6H 33
Barwell Cl. RG45: Crow 3B 24
Basemoors RG12: Brac 5E 9
Batcombe Mead
RG12: Brac 4E 17
Bathurst Rd. RG41: Winn 2A 4
Batty's Barn Cl.
RG40: Woki 1H 13
Bay Dr. RG12: Brac 5E 9
Bay Ho. RG12: Brac 5E 9
Bayley Ct. RG41: Winn 3A 4
Bay Rd. RG12: Brac 4E 9
Beale Cl. RG40: Woki 5F 5
Bean Oak Rd. RG40: Woki 6A 6
Bearsden Ct. SL5: S'dale 4B 20
Bearwood Lakes Golf Course
................1A 12
Bearwood Rd. RG41: Sind 5A 4
Beaufort Gdns. SL5: Asc 4C 10
Beaulieu Cl. RG12: Brac 6F 9
Beaulieu Gdns.
GU17: Blac 5E 35
Beaumont Gdns.
RG12: Brac 2E 17
Beaver Cl. RG41: Woki 3F 13
Beaver La. GU46: Yate 5A 34
Beckett Cl. RG40: Woki 6A 6
Beckford Av. RG12: Brac 3B 16
Beckford Cl. RG41: Woki 3D 4
Bedford Gdns. RG41: Woki ...5D 4
Bedford La. SL5: S'dale 2D 20
Bedfordshire Down
RG42: Warf 2F 9
Bedfordshire Way
RG41: Woki 6B 4
Beechbrook Av.
GU46: Yate 5A 34
Beechcroft Cl. SL5: S'hill 1H 19
Beechcroft Ct. RG12: Brac 6B 8
Beech Dr. GU17: Blac 6F 35
Beech Glen RG12: Brac 1B 16
Beech Hill Rd. SL5: S'dale ...3B 20
Beechnut Cl. RG41: Woki 1D 12
Beechnut Dr. GU17: Blac 4D 34
Beech Ride GU47: Sand 2D 34
Beech Wlk. GU20: Wind 4H 29
Beechwood Cl. SL5: Asc 3C 10
Beedon Dr. RG12: Brac 3G 15
Beehive La. RG12: Binf 5E 7
Beehive Rd. RG12: Binf 4F 7
BEGGAR'S BUSH 1B 20
Belfry M. GU47: Sand 2B 34
Bell Foundry La.
RG40: Woki 3F 5
Bell Ho. Gdns. RG41: Woki ...6F 5
(not continuous)
Bell La. GU17: Blac 5E 35
Bell Pl. GU19: Bag 5D 28
Belmont Rd. RG45: Crow 2D 24
Bembridge Ct.
RG45: Crow 4A 24
Benbricke Grn. RG42: Brac ...3A 8
Benedict Grn. RG42: Warf 3E 9
Benetfeld Rd. RG42: Binf 2D 6
Bennings Cl. RG42: Brac 3A 8
Benning Way RG40: Woki 4G 5
Benson Rd. RG45: Crow 3B 24
Bere Rd. RG12: Brac 3E 17
Berkshire Ct. RG12: Brac 5H 7
Berkshire Way RG12: Brac 6D 6
RG40: Woki 6D 6
Bernadine Cl. RG42: Warf 3E 9
Bernersh Cl. GU47: Sand 1E 35
Berrybank GU47: Coll T 4G 35
Berrycroft RG12: Brac 4D 8
Beryl Cl. RG41: Woki 5C 4
Beswick Gdns. RG12: Brac 4F 9
Beta Rd. GU24: Chob 3H 31
Betjeman Wlk. GU46: Yate ...6F 33
Bevan Ga. RG42: Brac 4A 8
Big Apple Leisure Cen. 1F 13
Big Barn Gro. RG42: Warf 3D 8
BILL HILL 1F 5
Billing Av. RG40: Finch 2C 22
Billingbear Cvn. Pk.
RG40: Woki 1B 6
Bilton Ind. Est.
RG12: Brac 1G 15
BINFIELD 2E 7
Binfield Rd. RG40: Woki 6A 6
RG42: Binf 2H 7
Binsted Dr. GU17: Blac 5F 35
Birch Ct. RG45: Crow 3B 24
Birch Dr. GU17: Haw 6F 35
Birches, The GU17: Blac 5D 34
Birchetts Cl. RG42: Brac 4B 8
Birch Gro. RG12: Brac 1C 16
BIRCH HILL 4B 16
Birch Hill Rd. RG12: Brac ...4B 16
Birchlands Ct. GU47: Owl ...6G 25
Birch La. SL5: Asc 4G 9
Birchmead RG41: Winn 2B 4
Birch Rd. GU20: Wind 4A 30
RG40: Finch 1D 22
Birch Side RG45: Crow 2B 24
Birchview Cl. GU46: Yate 6G 33
Bird M. RG40: Woki 6F 5
Birdwood Rd.
GU15: Camb 4G 35
Birkbeck Pl. GU47: Owl 1G 35
Birkdale RG12: Brac 4G 15
Bishopdale RG12: Brac 1A 16
Bishops Ct. SL5: Asc 2D 10
Bishop's Dr. RG40: Woki 5G 5
Bishops Gro. GU20: Wind 4G 29
Bittern Cl. GU47: Coll T 2F 35
Blackbird Cl. GU47: Coll T ...2F 35
Blackbushe Bus. Pk.
GU46: Yate 6G 33
Blackbushe Pk.
GU46: Yate 5G 33
Blackcap Pl. GU47: Coll T ...2G 35
Black Mdws. RG12: Brac 3C 16
Blackmoor Cl. SL5: Asc 5B 10
Blackmoor Wood SL5: Asc 5B 10
BLACKNEST 1D 20
Blacknest Rd.
GU25: Vir W 1G 21
SL5: S'hill 1G 21
BLACKWATER 6F 35
BLACKWATER PARK 6H 35
Blackwater Station (Rail) ...6G 35
Blackwater Valley Relief Rd.
GU15: Camb 6H 35
Blackwater Vw.
RG40: Finch 6F 23
Blagrove Dr. RG41: Woki 2D 12
Blagrove La. RG41: Woki 2D 12
Blaire Pk. GU46: Yate 2F 33
Blake Cl. RG40: Woki 4A 6
RG45: Crow 4E 25
Blakes Ride GU46: Yate 4F 33
Blamire Dr. RG42: Binf 2H 7
Blandford Dr. RG41: Woki ...2C 12
Blane's La. RG12: Brac 5F 17
SL5: Asc 5F 17
Blenheim Cl. RG41: Woki 6C 4
Blewburton Wlk.
RG12: Brac 1E 17
Blind La. GU24: Chob 6C 30
Blomfield Dale RG42: Brac 5F 7
Bloomfield Dr. RG12: Brac 3D 8
Bloomsbury Way
GU17: Haw 6F 35
Blount Cres. RG42: Binf 3G 7
Bloxworth Cl. RG12: Brac 1F 17
Bluebell Hill RG12: Brac 4E 9
Bluebell Mdw. RG41: Winn ...1A 4
Bluecoat Wlk. RG12: Brac ...2D 16
Bluethroat Cl.
GU47: Coll T 2G 35
Blythewood La. SL5: Asc 6C 10
Boden's Ride SL5: Asc 6B 18
(not continuous)
Bog La. RG12: Brac 2F 17
Boltons La. RG42: Binf 2G 7
Bond Way RG12: Brac 4B 8
Boole Hgts. RG12: Brac 3A 16
Booth Dr. RG40: Finch 5C 12
Borderside GU46: Yate 4E 33
Bosman Dr. GU20: Wind 1F 29
Bouldish Farm Rd.
SL5: Asc 2D 18
Boulevard, The RG12: Brac ...6F 7
Boulters Ho. RG12: Brac 1E 17
Bourneside GU25: Vir W 4H 21
Boveney Ho. *RG12: Brac 1E 17*
(off Segsbury Gro.)
Bowden Rd. SL5: S'hill 2G 19
Bowers, The RG40: Finch 5E 13
Bowland Dr. RG12: Brac 4E 17
Bowling Grn. Rd.
GU24: Chob 6G 31
Bowman Ct. RG45: Crow 4B 24
Bowyer Cres. RG40: Woki 4G 5
Bowyer Wlk. SL5: Asc 4C 10
Boxford Ridge RG12: Brac 6B 8
Boyd Ct. RG42: Brac 4A 8
Bracebridge GU15: Camb 5H 35
Bracken Bank SL5: Asc 4A 10
Bracken La. GU46: Yate 4E 33
Brackens, The
RG45: Crow 1C 24
SL5: Asc 6H 9
Bracken Way GU24: Chob ...3H 31
BRACKNELL 5C 8
Bracknell Beeches
RG12: Brac 6B 8
Bracknell Ent. Cen.
RG12: Brac 5A 8
Bracknell Rd. GU15: Camb ...6F 27
GU19: Bag 2B 28
RG12: Brac 5F 17
RG42: Warf 1E 9
RG45: Crow 3E 25
Bracknell Sports & Leisure Cen.
................2C 16
Bracknell Station (Rail) 6B 8
Bradfields RG12: Brac 2D 16
Bradley Dr. RG40: Woki 4E 13
Braeside RG12: Binf 5E 7
Brakes Ri. GU47: Coll T 2G 35
Bramblegate RG45: Crow 2C 24
Brambles, The
RG45: Crow 2H 23
Bramley Ct. RG45: Crow 3H 23
Bramley Gro. RG45: Crow ...3H 23
Bramley La. GU17: Blac 5D 34
Bramling Av. GU46: Yate 4F 33
Bramshill Rd. RG27: Ever ...3A 32
Branksome Hill Rd.
GU47: Coll T 3G 35
Brants Bri. RG12: Brac 5E 9
Brattain Ct. RG12: Brac 6D 8
Braybrooke Rd. RG42: Brac ...3B 8
Braye Cl. GU47: Sand 1E 35
Braziers La.
RG42: Wink R 1B 10
Bredon Rd. RG41: Woki 3D 4
Breech, The GU47: Coll T ...3G 35
Briarwood RG40: Finch 2C 22
Brickfield Cotts.
RG45: Crow 5B 24
Brickfields Ind. Pk.
RG12: Brac 5H 7

A-Z Bracknell 37

Clayhill Cl.—Easthampstead Rd.

Clayhill Cl. RG12: Brac 6F **9**
Clay La. RG40: Woki 6B **6**
Clayton Gro. RG12: Brac 4E **9**
Cleopatra Pl. RG42: Warf 3E **9**
Cleve Ho. RG12: Brac 1E **17**
Clifton Rd. RG41: Woki 4E **5**
Clintons Grn. RG42: Brac 4A **8**
Clive Grn. RG12: Brac 2B **16**
(not continuous)
Close, The GU18: Ligh 6E **29**
GU47: Coll T 2G **35**
RG12: Brac 1C **16**
SL5: Asc 5B **10**
Clover Cl. RG40: Woki 5A **6**
Clover La. GU46: Yate 4E **33**
Club La. RG45: Crow 3F **25**
Coachmans Gro.
GU47: Sand 3D **34**
Coach Rd. SL5: Asc 3C **10**
(not continuous)
Cobbett's La. GU17: Blac 6B **34**
GU46: Yate 5B **34**
Cochrane Pl. GU20: Wind . . .3H **29**
Cock-A-Dobby GU47: Sand . . .1C **34**
Cockpit Path RG40: Woki 1G **13**
Coleridge Av. GU46: Yate 5A **34**
Coleridge Cl. RG45: Crow . . .4E **25**
College Cres.
GU47: Coll T 2G **35**
College Ride GU19: Bag 6G **27**
College Rd. GU47: Coll T 3G **35**
RG12: Brac 1C **16**
COLLEGE TOWN **4G 35**
Columbia Cen., The
RG12: Brac 5B **8**
Columbia Ct. RG40: Finch . . .6C **12**
Colwyn Cl. GU46: Yate 4G **33**
Comfrey Cl. RG40: Woki 4A **6**
Commonfield La.
RG40: Bark 6A **12**
Commons Rd. RG41: Woki . . .3D **4**
Compton Cl. GU47: Sand 1E **35**
RG12: Brac 3G **15**
Comsaye Wlk. RG12: Brac . . .2C **16**
Coney Grange RG42: Warf . . .2B **8**
Conifers, The RG45: Crow . . .1C **24**
Coningsby RG12: Brac 1C **16**
Connaught Cl. GU46: Yate . . .4F **33**
RG45: Crow 5B **24**
Connaught Rd. GU19: Bag . . .5A **28**
Constable Way
GU47: Coll T 4G **35**
Cooke Ri. RG42: Warf 2C **8**
Cookham Cl. GU47: Sand 1E **35**
Cookham Rd. RG12: Brac 5G **7**
Coombe La. SL5: S'hill 1G **19**
Coombe Pine RG12: Brac 3D **16**
Coombe Rd. GU46: Yate 3F **33**
Coombes La.
RG41: Bark, Woki 2A **12**
Cooper Rd. GU20: Wind 4H **29**
Cooper's Hill RG27: Ever 6B **32**
Coote Cl. RG42: Binf 1E **7**
Copenhagen Wlk.
RG45: Crow 4D **24**
Copper Beech RG42: Warf 4G **9**
Copperfield Av.
GU47: Owl 6G **25**
Coppice Gdns. GU46: Yate . . .5G **33**
RG45: Crow 3B **24**
Coppice Grn. RG42: Brac 3H **7**
(not continuous)
Coppid Beech La.
RG40: Woki 6C **6**
Copse, The RG12: Brac 6D **8**
Copse Dr. RG41: Woki 5E **5**
Copse La. GU46: Yate 2F **33**
Copse Way RG40: Finch 1C **22**
Coral Reef Leisure Pool **4D 16**
Cordelia Cft. RG42: Warf 4E **9**
Corfield Cl. RG40: Finch 5C **22**
Corfield Grn. RG41: Woki 4D **4**
Cormorant Pl.
GU47: Coll T 3F **35**
Cornbunting Cl.
GU47: Coll T 2F **35**
Corn Cft. RG42: Warf 3D **8**
Cornfields GU46: Yate 6F **33**
Cornflower Cl. RG41: Woki . . .5B **4**
Cornwall Cl. RG41: Woki 6B **4**
RG42: Warf 2F **9**
Coronation Rd.
GU46: Yate 3A **34**
SL5: Asc 4E **19**
Coronation Sq. RG40: Woki . . .5H **5**
Corsham Way RG45: Crow . . .3D **24**
Cotswold Rd. GU47: Sand . . .1B **34**
Cotterell Cl. RG42: Brac 3B **8**
Cottesmore RG12: Brac 4A **16**
County La. RG42: Warf 2D **8**
Course Rd. SL5: Asc 6E **11**
Courtney Pl. RG42: Binf 2E **7**
Courtyard, The RG12: Brac . . .5D **8**
RG40: Woki 1G **13**
Covert, The SL5: Asc 4F **19**
Covert La. RG12: Brac 1C **16**
Coves Farm Wood
RG42: Brac 5F **7**
Coworth Cl. SL5: S'dale 2D **20**
Coworth Rd. SL5: S'dale 2C **20**
Cox Grn. GU47: Coll T 4F **35**
Crail Cl. RG41: Woki 3E **13**
Crake Pl. GU47: Coll T 2F **35**
Cranbourne Towers
SL5: Asc 4B **10**
Crane Ct. GU47: Coll T 2F **35**
Cranford Pk. Dr.
GU46: Yate 4H **33**
Crawley Chase
RG42: Wink R 2H **9**
Crecy Cl. RG41: Woki 6C **4**
Cree's Mdw. GU20: Wind 4G **29**
Crescent, The GU17: Haw 6F **35**
GU46: Yate 3H **33**
RG12: Brac 1C **16**
Crescent Rd. RG40: Woki . . .1G **13**
Cressex Cl. RG42: Binf 2E **7**
Cressida Chase RG42: Warf . . .3E **9**
Cricketers La.
GU20: Wind 3H **29**
RG42: Warf 1G **9**
Cricket Fld. Gro.
RG45: Crow 4F **25**
CRICKET HILL **5H 33**
Cricket Hill GU46: Yate 6A **34**
RG40: Finch 6D **22**
Crisp Gdns. RG42: Binf 3G **7**
Crocker Cl. SL5: Asc 4D **10**
Crockford Pl. RG42: Binf 3H **7**
Crocus Way RG41: Woki 5B **4**
Croft, The GU46: Yate 3H **33**
RG40: Woki 1H **13**
RG42: Brac 3B **8**
Croft Cl. RG41: Woki 4E **13**
Crofters Cl. GU47: Sand 2C **34**
Croft La. GU46: Yate 3G **33**
Crofton Cl. RG12: Brac 2E **17**
Croft Rd. RG40: Woki 5E **13**
Cromwell Rd. SL5: Asc 1F **19**
Crondall End GU46: Yate 3G **33**
Crosby Gdns. GU46: Yate 3E **33**
Crossfell RG12: Brac 1A **16**
Cross Gates Cl. RG12: Brac . . .6F **9**
Cross Rd. SL5: S'dale 5B **20**
Cross St. RG40: Woki 6G **5**
Crossway RG12: Brac 5C **8**
Crown Hill Ct. SL5: Asc 2F **19**
Crown Pl. GU47: Owl 1G **35**
Crown Row RG12: Brac 3D **16**
CROWN WOOD **3D 16**
CROWTHORNE **3E 25**
Crowthorne Bus. Est.
RG45: Crow 1E **25**
Crowthorne Lodge
RG12: Brac 1B 16
(off Crowthorne Rd.)
Crowthorne Rd.
GU47: Sand 2C **34**
RG12: Brac 2A **16**
(Easthampstead)
RG12: Brac 6G **15**
(Hanworth)
RG45: Crow 2F **25**
Crowthorne Rd. Nth.
RG12: Brac 6B **8**
Crowthorne Station (Rail) . . .**4A 24**
Cruikshank Lea
GU47: Coll T 4G **35**
Crutchley Rd. RG40: Woki 5H **5**
Culham Ho. RG12: Brac 1E **17**
Cullen Cl. GU46: Yate 5G **33**
Culloden Way RG41: Woki 6C **4**
Culvercroft RG42: Binf 3G **7**
Culver Rd. GU47: Owl 1F **35**
Cumberland Dr. RG12: Brac . . .4D **8**
Cumberland Way
RG41: Woki 6B **4**
Cumnor Way RG12: Brac 1E **17**
Cunworth Ct. RG12: Brac 3H **15**
Curl Way RG41: Woki 1E **13**
Cypress Cl. RG40: Finch 6E **13**
Cypress Way GU17: Blac 5D **34**

D

Dalcross RG12: Brac 3E **17**
Dale Cl. SL5: S'dale 2C **20**
Dale Gdns. GU47: Sand 2C **34**
Dale Lodge Rd.
SL5: S'dale 2C **20**
Dalley Ct. GU47: Coll T 3F **35**
Danywern Dr. RG41: Winn 2A **4**
DARBY GREEN **4C 34**
Darby Grn. La. GU17: Blac . . .5C **34**
Darby Grn. Rd.
GU17: Blac 5C **34**
Darby Va. RG42: Warf 2B **8**
Dark Dale SL5: Asc 2G **17**
Dark La. GU20: Wind 4F **29**
Darleydale Cl. GU47: Owl 6F **25**
Dart Cl. RG40: Finch 2D **22**
Dartmouth Cl. RG12: Brac 6E **9**
Darwall Dr. SL5: Asc 5B **10**
Darwin Pl. RG12: Brac 1C **16**
Dashwood Cl. RG12: Brac 4D **8**
Davenport Rd. RG12: Brac 4E **9**
Daventry Ct. RG42: Brac 4B **8**
Davis Gdns. GU47: Coll T 3G **35**
Davis Way RG10: Hurst 1B **4**
Davy Cl. RG40: Woki 1G **13**
Dawnay Cl. SL5: Asc 4D **10**
Deacon Cl. RG40: Woki 4G **5**
Dean Gro. RG40: Woki 5G **5**
Deans Ct. GU20: Wind 5H **29**
Deansgate RG12: Brac 4B **16**
Deepdale RG12: Brac 1A **16**
Deepfield Rd. RG12: Brac 5D **8**
Deerhurst Av. RG41: Winn 2A **4**
Deer Rock Hill RG12: Brac . . .3C **16**
Defford Cl. RG41: Woki 3D **4**
Delane Dr. RG41: Winn 3A **4**
Dell, The GU46: Yate 5G **33**
Dell Cnr. RG12: Brac 5G **7**
Deller St. RG42: Binf 3H **7**
Dell Rd. RG40: Finch 5E **23**
Delta Cl. GU24: Chob 3H **31**
Delta Rd. GU24: Chob 3H **31**
Dene Cl. RG12: Brac 3C **8**
Denham Dr. GU46: Yate 5H **33**
Denham Gro. RG12: Brac 3C **16**
Denmark St. RG40: Woki 1G **13**
Denmead Ct. RG12: Brac 3E **17**
Denton Rd. RG40: Woki 6G **5**
Derbyshire Grn. RG42: Warf . . .3F **9**
Derwent Cl. RG41: Woki 6C **4**
Devenish Cl. SL5: S'hill 3H **19**
Devenish La. SL5: S'dale 5H **19**
Devenish Rd.
SL5: S'dale, S'hill 3G **19**
Devil's Highway, The
RG45: Crow 3A **24**
De Vitre Grn. RG40: Woki 5B **6**
Devon Chase RG42: Warf 2E **9**
Devon Cl. GU47: Coll T 3F **35**
RG41: Woki 6C **4**
Diamond Way RG41: Woki 5C **4**
Dianthus Pl. RG42: Wink R . . .2H **9**
Dickens Ct. RG41: Woki 6F **5**
Dickens Way GU46: Yate 5G **33**
Dieppe Cl. RG41: Woki 6C **4**
Ditchfield La. RG40: Finch . . .6C **12**
Ditchling RG12: Brac 4A **16**
Dittons, The RG40: Finch 2D **22**
Dodsells Well RG40: Woki . . .6D **12**
Doles Hill RG41: Woki 3B **12**
Doles La. RG41: Woki 2C **12**
Dolphin Cl. RG41: Winn 3A **4**
Dolphin Ct. RG12: Brac 1C **16**
Doman Rd. GU15: Camb 6H **35**
Doncastle Rd. RG12: Brac 6G **7**
Donnington Pl. RG41: Winn . . .2B **4**
Donnybrook RG12: Brac 4A **16**
Dormer Cl. RG45: Crow 3C **24**
Dorset Va. RG42: Warf 2E **9**
Dorset Way RG41: Woki 6C **4**
Dovedale Cl. GU47: Owl 6F **25**
Dowding Ct. RG45: Crow 2E **25**
DOWLESGREEN **5A 6**
Dowles Grn. RG40: Woki 4A **6**
Downmill Rd. RG12: Brac 5H **7**
Downshire Way RG12: Brac . . .5A **8**
(not continuous)
Downside RG12: Brac 6B **8**
Doyle Gdns. GU46: Yate 6G **33**
Drake Cl. RG12: Brac 2B **16**
RG40: Finch 1C **22**
Draycott RG12: Brac 2E **17**
Drayhorse Dr. GU19: Bag 6C **28**
Drayton Cl. RG12: Brac 5D **8**
Drey Ho. RG41: Woki 5D **4**
***Driftways** GU46: Yate 3H 33*
(off White Lion Way)
Droitwich Cl. RG12: Brac 6D **8**
Drovers Way RG12: Brac 6F **9**
Druce Wood SL5: Asc 4C **10**
Drummond Cl. RG12: Brac 4F **9**
Dry Arch Rd. SL5: S'dale 3B **20**
Dryden RG12: Brac 4A **16**
Duchess Cl. RG45: Crow 1D **24**
Dukes Covert GU19: Bag 2C **28**
Dukes Hill GU19: Bag 2C **28**
Dukeshill Rd. RG42: Brac 4B **8**
Duke's Ride RG45: Crow 4A **24**
Dukes Wood RG45: Crow 2D **24**
(not continuous)
Dumas Cl. GU46: Yate 5G **33**
Duncan Dr. RG40: Woki 1H **13**
Dundas Cl. RG12: Brac 1B **16**
Dunford Pl. RG42: Binf 3G **7**
Dungells Farm Cl.
GU46: Yate 6H **33**
Dungells La. GU46: Yate 6G **33**
Dunkirk Cl. RG41: Woki 6C **4**
Dunsmore Gdns.
GU46: Yate 5E **33**
Dunt La. RG10: Hurst 1C **4**
Durham Cl. RG41: Woki 6C **4**
Durham Rd. GU47: Owl 6G **25**
Durley Mead RG12: Brac 2F **17**
Durning Pl. SL5: Asc 6F **11**
Duval Pl. GU19: Bag 5C **28**
Dyer Rd. RG40: Woki 5A **6**

E

Eagle Cl. RG41: Woki 1D **12**
RG45: Crow 2C **24**
Eaglehurst Cotts.
RG42: Binf 1E **7**
Eagles Nest GU47: Sand 1C **34**
Earle Cft. RG42: Warf 3C **8**
Earleydene SL5: Asc 5F **19**
Earlswood RG12: Brac 4B **16**
Eastbury Ct. RG42: Brac 3H **7**
Eastbury Pk. RG41: Winn 2B **4**
Eastcote Pl. SL5: Asc 4B **10**
EASTERN INDUSTRIAL AREA
. . . . **5D 8**
Eastern La. RG45: Crow 4H **25**
Eastern Rd. RG12: Brac 5D **8**
East Grn. GU17: Blac 6E **35**
EASTHAMPSTEAD **2B 16**
Easthampstead Mobile Home Pk.
RG40: Woki 6E **15**
Easthampstead Pk.
Crematorium & Cemetery
RG40: Woki 4F **15**
Easthampstead Rd.
RG12: Brac 5A **8**
RG40: Woki 1H **13**

Gorrick Sq.—Holly Spring Cotts.

Gorrick Sq. RG41: Woki . . . 3F 13
Gorselands GU46: Yate . . . 6G 33
Gorse La. GU24: Chob . . . 5G 31
Gorse Pl. RG42: Wink R . . . 3H 9
Gorse Ride Nth.
RG40: Finch . . . 1C 22
Gorse Ride Sth.
RG40: Finch . . . 1C 22
Gough's La. RG12: Brac . . . 3D 8
Gough's Mdw.
GU47: Sand . . . 3D 34
Governor's Rd.
GU15: Camb . . . 4H 35
Govett Gro. GU20: Wind . . . 3H 29
Gower Pk. GU47: Coll T . . . 3F 35
Gracious Pond Rd.
GU24: Chob . . . 5H 31
Graham Rd. GU20: Wind . . . 4G 29
Grampian Rd. GU47: Sand . . . 6B 24
Grand Regency Hgts.
SL5: Asc . . . 5C 10
Grange, The GU24: Chob . . . 3G 31
Grange Av. RG45: Crow . . . 2D 24
Grange Rd. RG12: Brac . . . 4C 8
Grantham Cl. GU47: Owl . . . 1G 35
Grant Rd. RG45: Crow . . . 5E 25
Grant Wlk. SL5: S'dale . . . 5A 20
Grasmere Cl. RG41: Winn . . . 3A 4
Gray Pl. RG42: Brac . . . 4G 7
Grayshot Dr. GU17: Blac . . . 5E 35
GREAT HOLLANDS . . . 3H 15
Gt. Hollands Rd.
RG12: Brac . . . 3G 15
Gt. Hollands Sq.
RG12: Brac . . . 3H 15
Green, The GU17: Blac . . . 6E 35
GU46: Yate . . . 4F 33
RG12: Brac . . . 1B 16
RG41: Woki . . . 5C 4
Green Cft. RG40: Woki . . . 4A 6
Green Dr. RG40: Woki . . . 2A 14
Green End GU46: Yate . . . 3H 33
Green Farm Rd.
GU19: Bag . . . 5D 28
Greenfield Way
RG45: Crow . . . 1C 24
Grn. Finch Cl. RG45: Crow . . . 2B 24
Greenfinch Cl. GU47: Owl . . . 2F 35
Greenham Wood
RG12: Brac . . . 3C 16
Greenhaven GU46: Yate . . . 5F 33
Greenhow RG12: Brac . . . 6A 8
Green La. GU17: Blac . . . 6D 34
GU17: Haw . . . 6G 35
GU19: Bag . . . 1H 27
(Bagshot Rd.)
GU19: Bag . . . 6D 28
(Whitmoor Rd.)
GU24: Chob . . . 3H 31
GU46: Yate . . . 4F 33
GU47: Sand . . . 3E 35
RG10: Hurst . . . 1C 4
RG40: Woki . . . 1C 6
RG41: Winn . . . 3B 4
Greenleas Cl. GU46: Yate . . . 3G 33
Green Ride RG12: Brac . . . 4F 17
Greenside RG45: Crow . . . 3B 24
Greenways GU47: Sand . . . 1D 34
Greenways Dr. SL5: S'dale . . . 5A 20
Greenwood SL5: Asc . . . 4A 10
Greenwood Cotts.
SL5: S'dale . . . 3E 21
Greenwood Gro.
RG41: Winn . . . 1B 4
Greenwood Rd.
RG45: Crow . . . 2C 24
Grensell Cl. RG27: Ever . . . 2C 32
Grenville Pl. *RG12: Brac . . . 5C 8*
(off The Ring)
Greyfriars Dr. SL5: Asc . . . 2F 19
Greystock Rd. RG42: Warf . . . 2D 8
Greystoke Ct. RG45: Crow . . . 4C 24
Grove, The SL5: Asc . . . 4A 10
Grove Cl. RG40: Woki . . . 1A 24
Grove End GU19: Bag . . . 4D 28
Grovelands Av. RG41: Winn . . . 2B 4
Grovelands Av. Workshops
RG41: Winn . . . 1B 4
Grovelands Cl. RG41: Winn . . . 1B 4
Grovelands Pk. *RG41: Winn . . . 1B 4*
(off Grovelands Av.)
Grove La. RG42: Wink R . . . 1H 9
Guards Ct. SL5: S'dale . . . 4D 20
Guerdon Pl. RG12: Brac . . . 4D 16
Guildford Rd. GU18: Ligh . . . 6E 29
GU19: Bag, Ligh . . . 5C 28
(not continuous)
Gull Cl. RG41: Woki . . . 1C 12

H

Haddenhurst Ct. RG42: Binf . . . 2E 7
Haig Rd. GU15: Camb . . . 4H 35
Hailsham Cl. GU47: Owl . . . 1F 35
Halebourne La.
GU24: Chob . . . 5C 30
Hale End RG12: Brac . . . 1F 17
Halewood RG12: Brac . . . 3H 15
Half Moon St. GU19: Bag . . . 5C 28
Halfpenny La. SL5: S'dale . . . 4C 20
Hallbrooke Gdns.
RG42: Binf . . . 3G 7
Halley Dr. SL5: Asc . . . 5B 10
Hall Farm Cres.
GU46: Yate . . . 5H 33
Hallgrove Bottom
GU19: Bag . . . 3D 28
Hall Gro. Farm Ind. Est.
GU19: Bag . . . 3D 28
Hall La. GU46: Yate . . . 5G 33
Hallmark Cl. GU47: Coll T . . . 2G 35
Hamble Av. GU17: Blac . . . 5F 35
Hambleden Ct.
RG12: Brac . . . 1E 17
Hamilton Cl. GU19: Bag . . . 5C 28
Hamilton Dr. SL5: S'dale . . . 4A 20
Hamlet St. RG42: Warf . . . 4E 9
Hammond Ct. *RG42: Brac . . . 4A 8*
(off Crescent Rd.)
Hammond Way
GU18: Ligh . . . 6F 29
Hampshire Ri. RG42: Warf . . . 2F 9
Hampshire Way
RG41: Woki . . . 6B 4
Hampstead Rd.
RG40: Woki . . . 4C 14
Hancocks Mt. SL5: S'hill . . . 3H 19
Hancombe Rd.
GU47: Sand . . . 1C 34
Handford La. GU46: Yate . . . 5H 33
Hangerfield Cl.
GU46: Yate . . . 5G 33
Hanover Cl. GU46: Yate . . . 3H 33
Hanover Gdns.
RG12: Brac . . . 4H 15
Hanover Pk. SL5: Asc . . . 4D 10
HANWORTH . . . 4A 16
Hanworth Cl. RG12: Brac . . . 3C 16
Hanworth Rd. RG12: Brac . . . 5A 16
Harcourt Rd. RG12: Brac . . . 3B 16
Hardwell Way RG12: Brac . . . 1E 17
Hardy Av. GU46: Yate . . . 6G 33
Hardy Grn. RG45: Crow . . . 4D 24
Harefield Cl. RG41: Winn . . . 2A 4
Harlech Rd. GU17: Haw . . . 6F 35
Harman Ct. RG41: Winn . . . 2A 4
HARMANS WATER . . . 1E 17
Harman's Water Rd.
RG12: Brac . . . 2C 16
Harmanswater Sports Cen. . . . 2E 17
Harmar Cl. RG40: Woki . . . 6A 6
Harpton Cl. GU46: Yate . . . 3H 33
Harpton Pde. GU46: Yate . . . 3H 33
Hart Cl. RG42: Brac . . . 3B 8
Hart Dene Ct. GU19: Bag . . . 5C 28
Hart Dyke Cl. RG41: Woki . . . 4F 13
Hartley Cl. GU17: Blac . . . 5D 34
Hart M. GU46: Yate . . . 4F 33
Harts Leap Cl.
GU47: Sand . . . 1D 34
Harts Leap Rd.
GU47: Sand . . . 2C 34
Harvard Rd. GU47: Owl . . . 1G 35
Harvest Cl. GU46: Yate . . . 6F 33
Harvest Dr. RG41: Sind . . . 4A 4
Harvest Lea RG42: Warf . . . 4G 9
Harvest Ride RG42: Warf . . . 2A 8
Hatch End GU20: Wind . . . 4G 29
Hatchet La. SL4: Wink . . . 1E 11
SL5: Asc . . . 1E 11
Hatchgate Copse
RG12: Brac . . . 3G 15
Hatch Ride RG40: Woki . . . 6B 14
RG45: Crow . . . 6C 14
Hatherwood GU46: Yate . . . 5B 34
HATTON HILL . . . 3G 29
Hatton Hill GU20: Wind . . . 2F 29
Havelock Rd. RG41: Woki . . . 6E 5
Havelock St. RG41: Woki . . . 6E 5
Haversham Dr. RG12: Brac . . . 3B 16
Hawkes Cl. RG41: Woki . . . 5E 5
Hawkes Leap GU20: Wind . . . 2F 29
Hawkesworth Dr.
GU19: Bag . . . 6B 28
Hawkins Cl. GU46: Yate . . . 5F 33
RG12: Brac . . . 5G 9
Hawkins Way RG40: Woki . . . 6A 6
Hawk La. RG12: Brac . . . 1D 16
Hawkridge Ct. RG12: Brac . . . 1E 17
Hawkswood Ho.
RG42: Brac . . . 4G 7
(off Moordale Av.)
Hawley Rd. GU17: Haw . . . 6F 35
Hawthorn Cl. RG42: Brac . . . 4A 8
Hawthorne Cres.
GU17: Haw . . . 6G 35
Haydon Pl. GU46: Yate . . . 4A 34
Hayes La. RG41: Woki . . . 3A 12
Hayley Grn. RG42: Warf . . . 1F 9
Haywood RG12: Brac . . . 4C 16
Hazelbank RG40: Finch . . . 2C 22
Hazel Cl. RG41: Woki . . . 1D 12
Hazell Hill RG12: Brac . . . 6C 8
Hazelwood La.
RG42: Binf, Warf . . . 1H 7
Headington Cl. RG40: Woki . . . 4H 5
Headington Dr. RG40: Woki . . . 4H 5
Hearmon Cl. GU46: Yate . . . 4A 34
Hearn Wlk. RG12: Brac . . . 4E 9
Hearsey Gdns. GU17: Blac . . . 4D 34
(not continuous)
Heath Cl. RG41: Woki . . . 2E 13
Heath Ct. GU19: Bag . . . 5C 28
Heather Cl. RG40: Finch . . . 1C 22
Heatherdene Av.
RG45: Crow . . . 4A 24
Heather Dr. SL5: S'dale . . . 4D 20
Heathermount RG12: Brac . . . 1E 17
Heathermount Dr.
RG45: Crow . . . 2B 24
Heathermount Gdns.
RG45: Crow . . . 2B 24
Heather Way GU24: Chob . . . 5G 31
Heatherway RG45: Crow . . . 3C 24
HEATHERWOOD HOSPITAL . . . 6C 10
Heathfield Av. SL5: S'dale . . . 2A 20
Heath Hill Rd. Nth.
RG45: Crow . . . 3D 24
Heath Hill Rd. Sth.
RG45: Crow . . . 3D 24
Heathlands RG12: Brac . . . 1A 16
Heathlands Ct. GU46: Yate . . . 6A 34
RG40: Woki . . . 6B 14
Heathlands Rd.
RG40: Woki . . . 3B 14
Heathmoors RG12: Brac . . . 2C 16
Heathpark Dr. GU20: Wind . . . 4A 30
Heath Pl. GU19: Bag . . . 5C 28
Heath Ride RG40: Finch . . . 2E 23
RG45: Crow . . . 3G 23
Heath Rd. GU19: Bag . . . 5C 28
Heathway SL5: Asc . . . 4C 10
Heathwood Cl. GU46: Yate . . . 3H 33
Hebbecastle Down
RG42: Warf . . . 2B 8
Hedge Cft. GU46: Yate . . . 4F 33
Hedge La. RG42: Warf . . . 2D 8
Heelas Rd. RG41: Woki . . . 6E 5
Helmsdale RG12: Brac . . . 2D 16
Hemmyng Cnr. RG42: Warf . . . 2C 8
Henley Gdns. GU46: Yate . . . 5H 33
Hepworth Cft.
GU47: Coll T . . . 4G 35
Herbert Cl. RG12: Brac . . . 2B 16
Hermes Cl. RG41: Woki . . . 5A 4
Hermitage, The
RG42: Warf . . . 1D 8
Hermitage Dr. SL5: Asc . . . 5C 10
Hermitage Pde. SL5: Asc . . . 6E 11
Heron Cl. SL5: Asc . . . 4B 10
Heron Ct. GU47: Sand . . . 3E 35
Herondale RG12: Brac . . . 4C 16
Heron Rd. RG41: Woki . . . 6C 4
Heron's Way RG40: Woki . . . 5A 6
Herrings La. GU20: Wind . . . 3H 29
Herriot Ct. GU46: Yate . . . 6G 33
Herschel Grange
RG42: Warf . . . 1D 8
Hertford Cl. RG41: Woki . . . 1C 12
Hewlett Pl. GU19: Bag . . . 5D 28
Hexham Cl. GU47: Owl . . . 6F 25
Heywood Dr. GU19: Bag . . . 6A 28
Hicks La. GU17: Blac . . . 5D 34
Higgs La. GU19: Bag . . . 5B 28
(not continuous)
Highams La. GU24: Chob . . . 4C 30
High Beech RG12: Brac . . . 1F 17
Highclere SL5: S'hill . . . 2H 19
Highclere Cl. RG12: Brac . . . 5E 9
High Cl. *RG40: Woki . . . 5G 5*
(off Wiltshire Rd.)
Higher Alham RG12: Brac . . . 4E 17
Highfield RG12: Brac . . . 3H 15
Highfield Cl. RG40: Woki . . . 6F 5
High Flds. SL5: S'dale . . . 2B 20
Highgrove Av. SL5: Asc . . . 4D 10
Highland Av. RG41: Woki . . . 1A 12
High St. GU19: Bag . . . 5C 28
GU24: Chob . . . 4G 31
GU47: Sand . . . 1B 34
(Church Rd.)
GU47: Sand . . . 1B 34
(Mountbatten Ri.)
RG12: Brac . . . 5B 8
(not continuous)
RG45: Crow . . . 4E 25
SL5: Asc . . . 6C 10
SL5: S'dale . . . 2C 20
SL5: S'hill . . . 2H 19
Highway RG45: Crow . . . 3C 24
Highwayman's Ridge
GU20: Wind . . . 2F 29
Highwood Cl. GU46: Yate . . . 6G 33
Hilfield GU46: Yate . . . 5B 34
Hillary Dr. RG45: Crow . . . 2D 24
Hillberry RG12: Brac . . . 4C 16
Hill Copse Vw. RG12: Brac . . . 4E 9
Hillhampton Pl.
SL5: S'dale . . . 4B 20
Hillside GU15: Camb . . . 3H 35
SL5: S'hill . . . 2G 19
Hillside Dr. RG42: Binf . . . 2E 7
Hillside Pk. SL5: S'dale . . . 5B 20
Hilltop Cl. SL5: Asc . . . 5H 11
Hilltop Vw. GU46: Yate . . . 5F 33
Hinton Cl. RG45: Crow . . . 1D 24
Hinton Dr. RG45: Crow . . . 1D 24
Hitherhooks Hill RG42: Binf . . . 4G 7
Hodge La. SL4: Wink . . . 1E 11
(not continuous)
Hodges Cl. GU19: Bag . . . 6B 28
Hoffman Cl. RG42: Brac . . . 2D 8
Hogarth Cl. GU47: Coll T . . . 4G 35
Holbeche Cl. GU46: Yate . . . 4E 33
Holbeck RG12: Brac . . . 3H 15
Holland Pines RG12: Brac . . . 4H 15
Hollerith Ri. RG12: Brac . . . 3B 16
Holly Acre GU46: Yate . . . 5H 33
Hollybush La. RG27: Ever . . . 2C 32
Hollybush Ride
GU20: Wind . . . 1D 28
RG40: Finch . . . 3G 23
RG45: Crow . . . 4G 23
Holly Cl. RG27: Ever . . . 3C 32
Holly Ct. RG45: Crow . . . 4A 24
Hollyhook Cl. RG45: Crow . . . 2C 24
Holly Ho. RG12: Brac . . . 3B 16
Holly Spring Cotts.
RG12: Brac . . . 3D 8

Holly Spring La.—Linkway

Holly Spring La.
RG12: Brac 4C **8**
Holly Way GU17: Blac 6F **35**
Hollywood Bowl
Bracknell 5B **8**
Holmbury Av. RG45: Crow . . .1C **24**
Holme Cl. RG45: Crow 1C **24**
HOLME GREEN **3B 14**
Holmes Cl. RG41: Woki 2D **12**
SL5: S'hill 3G **19**
Holmes Cres. RG41: Woki . . .2D **12**
Holmewood Cl.
RG41: Woki 4E **13**
Holt La. RG41: Woki 5F **5**
Holton Heath RG12: Brac 1F **17**
Hombrook Dr. RG42: Brac 4G **7**
Hombrook Ho. RG42: Brac 4G **7**
Home Pk. Rd. GU46: Yate . . .4H **33**
Hone Hill GU47: Sand 2D **34**
Honey Hill RG40: Woki 4B **14**
HONEYHILL **5B 14**
Honeyhill Rd. RG42: Brac 4A **8**
Honeysuckle Cl.
GU46: Yate 4E **33**
RG45: Crow 1C **24**
Hook Mill La. GU18: Ligh . . .6H **29**
Hope Av. RG12: Brac 4E **17**
Hope Cotts. RG12: Brac 6C **8**
Hopeman Cl. GU47: Coll T . . .2F **35**
Hopper Va. RG12: Brac 3A **16**
Horatio Av. RG42: Warf 4E **9**
Horewood Rd. RG12: Brac . . .3B **16**
Hormer Cl. GU47: Owl 1F **35**
Hornbeam Cl. GU47: Owl 1F **35**
RG41: Woki 3B **12**
Hornbeam Copse
RG42: Warf 4G **9**
Hornby Av. RG12: Brac 4D **16**
Horndean Rd. RG12: Brac . . .3F **17**
Horsebrass Dr. GU19: Bag . . .6C **28**
Horsegate Ride SL5: Asc 3E **19**
(Coronation Rd.)
SL5: Asc 2H **17**
(Swinley Rd.)
Horseshoe Lake Watersports Cen.
. . . . .1H **33**
Horsham Rd. GU47: Owl 1F **35**
Horsnape Gdns. RG42: Binf . . .2D **6**
Horsneile La. RG42: Brac 3B **8**
Houlton Ct. GU19: Bag 6C **28**
Houston Way RG45: Crow . . .3H **23**
Howard Cl. RG12: Brac 2A **16**
Howard Rd. RG40: Woki 1G **13**
Howell Cl. RG42: Warf 2C **8**
Howorth Ct. RG12: Brac 1F **17**
Hubberholme RG12: Brac 6A **8**
Huddington Glade
GU46: Yate 5E **33**
Hughes Rd. RG40: Woki 5H **5**
Humber Cl. GU47: Sand 2F **35**
RG41: Woki 5C **4**
Humber Way GU47: Sand 2F **35**
Humphries Yd.
RG12: Brac 1C **16**
Hungerford Cl.
GU47: Sand 2E **35**
Huntingdonshire Cl.
RG41: Woki 6B **4**
Huntsgreen Ct. RG12: Brac . . .5C **8**
Huntsmans Mdw.
SL5: Asc 4D **10**
Hurley Ct. RG12: Brac 1E **17**
Hurst Cl. RG12: Brac 2A **16**
Hurstwood SL5: Asc 3E **19**
Huson Rd. RG42: Warf 2C **8**
Hutsons Cl. RG40: Woki 4H **5**
Hutton Cl. GU20: Wind 5H **29**
Hythe Cl. RG12: Brac 2E **17**

I

Ilex Cl. GU46: Yate 4F **33**
Illingworth Gro. RG12: Brac . . .4F **9**
Imperial College London . . .**1B 20**
Inchwood RG12: Brac 5C **16**
Ingle Glen RG40: Finch 1E **23**
Ingleton RG12: Brac 6A **8**
Ink, The GU46: Yate 3G **33**
Innings La. RG42: Warf 4D **8**
Inverness Way
GU47: Coll T 3F **35**
Isis Way GU47: Sand 2F **35**
Iveagh Ct. RG12: Brac 2D **16**
Ives Cl. GU46: Yate 3F **33**

J

Jackson Cl. RG12: Brac 2B **16**
Jacob Cl. RG42: Brac 5F **7**
Jacob Rd. GU15: Camb 3H **35**
Jameston RG12: Brac 5C **16**
Japonica Cl. RG41: Woki 2B **12**
Jarvis Cl. RG27: Ever 2C **32**
Jasmine Cl. RG41: Woki 5B **4**
Jays Nest Cl. GU17: Blac 6F **35**
Jenkins Ct. GU19: Bag 6B **28**
Jenkins Hill GU19: Bag 6B **28**
Jennys Wlk. GU46: Yate 4A **34**
Jerome Cnr. RG45: Crow 5E **25**
Jerrymoor Hill
RG40: Finch 6D **12**
Jersey Pl. SL5: S'hill 3H **19**
Jesse Cl. GU46: Yate 5B **34**
Jevington RG12: Brac 5C **16**
Jig's La. Nth. RG42: Warf 2E **9**
Jig's La. Sth. RG42: Warf 4E **9**
Jock's La. RG42: Brac 4G **7**
John Nike Leisuresport Complex
. . . . .5E **7**
John Nike Way RG12: Brac . . .5E **7**
John Pl. RG42: Warf 3E **9**
Johnson Dr. RG40: Finch 1F **23**
Jones Cnr. SL5: Asc 4C **10**
Joseph Ct. RG42: Warf 2E **9**
Jubilee Av. RG41: Woki 5F **5**
SL5: Asc 4C **10**
Jubilee Cl. SL5: Asc 4C **10**
Jubilee Ct. RG12: Brac 6C **8**
SL5: Asc 3C **10**
Jubilee Rd. RG40: Finch 3D **22**
Juliet Gdns. RG42: Warf 4F **9**
Julius Hill RG42: Warf 4F **9**
Juniper RG12: Brac 5C **16**
Junipers, The RG41: Woki . . .2B **12**
Jupiter Way RG41: Woki 6C **4**
Jutland Cl. RG41: Woki 6C **4**

K

Kaynes Pk. SL5: Asc 4C **10**
Keates Grn. RG42: Brac 4B **8**
Keats Way GU46: Yate 6F **33**
RG45: Crow 1D **24**
Keble Way GU47: Owl 6G **25**
Keeble Ho. RG41: Woki 6E **5**
Keepers Coombe
RG12: Brac 3D **16**
Keephatch Rd. RG40: Woki . . .4A **6**
Kelburne Cl. RG41: Winn 1A **4**
Keldholme RG12: Brac 6A **8**
Kelsall Pl. SL5: Asc 4F **19**
Kelsey Av. RG40: Finch 2C **22**
Kelsey Gro. GU46: Yate 5A **34**
Kelvin Ga. RG12: Brac 5D **8**
Kemp Ct. GU19: Bag 6D **28**
Kendrick Cl. RG40: Woki 1G **13**
Kenilworth Av. RG12: Brac 4C **8**
Kennel Av. SL5: Asc 4D **10**
Kennel Cl. SL5: Asc 2D **10**
Kennel Grn. SL5: Asc 4C **10**
Kennel La. GU20: Wind 3G **29**
RG42: Brac 3B **8**
Kennel Ride SL5: Asc 4D **10**
Kennel Wood SL5: Asc 4D **10**
Kennet Ct. RG41: Woki 6D **4**
Kent Cl. RG41: Woki 1B **12**
Kent Folly RG42: Warf 2F **9**
Kentigern Dr. RG45: Crow 3F **25**
Kenton Cl. RG12: Brac 5D **8**
Kent Rd. GU20: Wind 3H **29**
Kenworth Gro. GU18: Ligh . . .6E **29**
Kepple Pl. GU19: Bag 5C **28**
Kesteven Way RG41: Woki 6C **4**
Kestrel Way RG41: Woki 6C **4**
Ketcher Grn. RG42: Binf 1E **7**
Kevins Dr. GU46: Yate 3A **34**
Keynsham Way GU47: Owl . . .6F **25**
Kibble Grn. RG12: Brac 3C **16**
Kier Pk. SL5: Asc 6G **11**
Killy Hill GU24: Chob 5G **31**
Kilmington Cl. RG12: Brac . . .4E **17**
Kilmuir Cl. GU47: Coll T 3F **35**
Kiln La. RG12: Brac 5A **8**
SL4: Wink 2F **11**
SL5: S'dale 2C **20**
Kiln Ride RG40: Finch 6E **13**
Kiln Ride Extension
RG40: Finch 2E **23**
Kilometre, The
RG45: Crow 4B **24**
Kimberley RG12: Brac 5C **16**
Kimmeridge RG12: Brac 3E **17**
King Edward's Cl.
SL5: Asc 4C **10**
King Edward's Ri.
SL5: Asc 3C **10**
King Edward's Rd.
SL5: Asc 4C **10**
Kingfisher Dr. GU46: Yate 4F **33**
Kingsbridge Cotts.
RG40: Woki 1H **23**
Kings Glade GU46: Yate 4B **34**
King's Keep GU47: Sand 1D **34**
Kings La. GU20: Wind 3A **30**
Kingsley Cl. RG45: Crow 5D **24**
Kingsley Rd. RG27: Ever 3A **32**
Kingsmere Rd. RG42: Brac . . .4H **7**
King's Ride GU15: Camb 6D **26**
SL5: Asc 2A **18**
Kings Ride Pk. SL5: Asc 2A **18**
King's Rd. RG45: Crow 4D **24**
SL5: S'dale, S'hill 2H **19**
King St. La. RG41: Winn 3A **4**
King's Wlk. GU15: Camb 4H **35**
Kingsway GU17: Blac 5F **35**
Kingswick Cl. SL5: S'hill 1A **20**
Kingswick Dr. SL5: S'hill 1H **19**
Kingswood SL5: Asc 1A **18**
Kings Yd. SL5: Asc 1C **18**
Kinross Av. SL5: Asc 2D **18**
Kinross Ct. SL5: Asc 2D **18**
Kipling Cl. GU46: Yate 6G **33**
Kipling Hall RG45: Crow 3D **24**
Kirkham Cl. GU47: Owl 6F **25**
Knightswood RG12: Brac 5B **16**
Knole Wood SL5: S'dale 5A **20**
Knook, The GU47: Coll T 3F **35**
Knowles Av. RG45: Crow 3B **24**
Knox Grn. RG42: Binf 1E **7**
Kyle Cl. RG12: Brac 6B **8**

L

Laburnum Rd. RG41: Winn . . .3A **4**
Laburnums, The
GU17: Blac 5D **34**
Ladybank RG12: Brac 5B **16**
Lady Margaret Rd.
SL5: S'dale 5B **20**
Laird Ct. GU19: Bag 6C **28**
Lake End Way
RG45: Crow 4C **24**
Lakeside RG42: Brac 3C **8**
Lakeside, The GU17: Blac . . .6F **35**
Lakeside Bus. Pk.
GU47: Sand 3C **34**
Lalande Cl. RG41: Woki 6C **4**
Lambert Cres. GU17: Blac . . .6E **35**
Lamborne Cl. GU47: Sand . . .1C **34**
Lambourne Dr. GU19: Bag . . .6B **28**
Lambourne Gro.
RG12: Brac 5E **9**
Lammas Mead RG42: Binf 3G **7**
Lancashire Hill RG42: Warf . . .2F **9**
Lancaster Ho. RG12: Brac . . .2B **16**
Lanchester Dr.
RG45: Crow 1E **25**
Landen Ct. RG40: Woki 2F **13**
Landen Gro. RG41: Woki 4C **4**
Landseer Cl. GU47: Coll T . . .4G **35**
Langborough Rd.
RG40: Woki 1G **13**
Langdale Dr. SL5: Asc 5C **10**
Larch Av. RG41: Woki 5E **5**
SL5: S'dale 2A **20**
Larches, The RG42: Warf 3G **9**
Larches Way GU17: Blac 5D **34**
Larchwood RG12: Brac 2F **17**
Larges Bri. Dr. RG12: Brac . . .6C **8**
Larges La. RG12: Brac 5C **8**
Larkspur Cl. RG41: Woki 5B **4**
Larkswood Cl. GU47: Sand . . .1C **34**
Larkswood Dr.
RG45: Crow 3D **24**
Latimer RG12: Brac 5B **16**
Latimer Rd. RG41: Woki 1F **13**
Laud Way RG40: Woki 6A **6**
Laundry La. GU47: Coll T 4G **35**
Lauradale RG12: Brac 1A **16**
Laurel Bank *GU24: Chob 4G 31*
(off Bagshot Rd.)
Laurel Cl. RG41: Woki 1D **12**
Laurel Ct. *RG12: Brac 1F 17*
(off Wayland Clo.)
Lawford Cres. GU46: Yate . . .4H **33**
Lawns, The SL5: Asc 6B **10**
Lawrence Cen.
RG41: Woki 2E **13**
Lawrence Cl. RG40: Woki 6H **5**
Lawrence Cres.
GU20: Wind 4H **29**
Lawrence Gro. RG42: Binf 4F **7**
Lawrence Way
GU15: Camb 6H **35**
Lawson Way SL5: S'dale 3D **20**
Lea, The RG40: Woki 6D **12**
Lea Cft. RG45: Crow 2D **24**
Leacroft SL5: S'dale 2C **20**
Leafield Copse RG12: Brac . . .1F **17**
Leaves Grn. RG12: Brac 3D **16**
Leicester RG12: Brac 4E **17**
Leith Cl. RG45: Crow 1C **24**
Lemington Gro.
RG12: Brac 3B **16**
Leney Cl. RG40: Woki 4H **5**
Lenham Cl. RG41: Winn 3C **4**
Leppington RG12: Brac 5B **16**
Leslie Rd. GU24: Chob 3G **31**
Letcombe Sq. RG12: Brac . . .1E **17**
Leverkusen Rd.
RG12: Brac 6B **8**
Lewisham Way GU47: Owl . . .1F **35**
Lewis Ho. RG12: Brac 3B **16**
Leycester Cl. GU20: Wind . . .2F **29**
Leyside RG45: Crow 3C **24**
Lichfields RG12: Brac 5E **9**
Liddell Cl. RG40: Finch 5C **22**
Liddell Way SL5: Asc 2D **18**
Lightwater By-Pass
GU18: Ligh 6E **29**
Lightwood RG12: Brac 3D **16**
Lilacs, The RG41: Woki 3A **12**
Lilley Ct. RG45: Crow 4D **24**
Lily Ct. RG41: Woki 6F **5**
Lily Hill Dr. RG12: Brac 5E **9**
Lily Hill Rd. RG12: Brac 5E **9**
Lime Av. SL5: Asc 3H **17**
Lime Cl. RG41: Woki 1D **12**
Limecroft GU46: Yate 5G **33**
Limerick Cl. RG42: Brac 4A **8**
Limes, The RG42: Warf 1F **9**
Lime Tree Copse
RG42: Warf 3G **9**
Lime Wlk. RG12: Brac 1C **16**
Limmer Cl. RG41: Woki 2A **12**
LIMMERHILL **1C 12**
Limmerhill Rd.
RG41: Woki 1C **12**
Lincolnshire Gdns.
RG42: Warf 3E **9**
Lindale Cl. GU25: Vir W 1H **21**
Linden RG12: Brac 2F **17**
Linden Cl. RG41: Woki 1D **12**
Lindenhill Rd. RG42: Brac 4H **7**
Lindsey Cl. RG41: Woki 6C **4**
Lingwood RG12: Brac 3C **16**
Links, The SL5: Asc 5C **10**
Linkway RG45: Crow 3B **24**

42 A-Z Bracknell

Linnet Wlk.—Mt. Pleasant

Linnet Wlk. RG41: Woki 6C 4
Liscombe RG12: Brac 4B 16
Liscombe Ho. RG12: Brac . . .4B 16
Little Copse GU46: Yate 3H 33
Little Cft. GU46: Yate 5H 33
Littledale Cl. RG12: Brac 6E 9
Little Foxes RG40: Finch 1E 23
Little Fryth RG40: Finch 2G 23
Lit. Heath Rd.
GU24: Chob 6G 31
Lit. Hill Rd. RG10: Hurst 1B 4
Little Moor GU47: Sand 1E 35
Little Ringdale RG12: Brac . . .1E 17
LITTLE SANDHURST **6C 24**
Little Vigo GU46: Yate 6F 33
Llangar Gro. RG45: Crow 3C 24
Llanvair Cl. SL5: Asc 3E 19
Llanvair Dr. SL5: Asc 3D 18
Lochinver RG12: Brac 4B 16
Locks Ride SL5: Asc 4H 9
Lockton Chase SL5: Asc 6B 10
Lodge Gro. GU46: Yate 4B 34
Lodges, The RG40: Finch 1D 22
London Rd. GU17: Blac 6F 35
GU19: Bag 6A 28
GU20: Wind 2E 29
GU25: Vir W 2E 21
RG12: Binf 5D 6
RG12: Brac 5D 8
RG40: Woki 6H 5
RG42: Binf 5D 6
SL5: Asc 6G 9
SL5: Asc, S'hill 6F 11
SL5: S'dale 2E 29
Loneacre GU20: Wind 4A 30
LONGCROSS **1H 31**
Longcross Rd.
GU24: Chob 1H 31
KT16: Long 1H 31
Longcross Station (Rail) **5H 21**
Longdon Rd. RG41: Winn 3A 4
Longdown Lodge
GU47: Sand 2D 34
Longdown Rd.
GU47: Sand 1C 34
Long Hill Rd. SL5: Asc 5G 9
Long La. RG40: Woki 2B 6
Long Mickle GU47: Sand 1C 34
Longmoor Cl. RG40: Finch . . .2C 22
Longmoors RG42: Brac 4G 7
Longshot Ind. Est.
RG12: Brac 5G 7
Longshot La. RG12: Brac 6G 7
(not continuous)
Long's Way RG40: Woki 5A 6
Longwater La. RG27: Ever . . .2C 32
RG40: Finch 5D 22
Longwater Rd. RG12: Brac . . .3C 16
RG40: Finch 1C 32
Look Out, The (Heritage Cen.)
. . . .**5D 16**
Lory Ridge GU19: Bag 4C 28
Loughborough RG12: Brac . . .3E 17
Lovedean Ct. RG12: Brac 3E 17
Lovelace Rd. RG12: Brac 1G 15
Love La. GU46: Yate 4E 33
Lovel La. SL4: Wink 1E 11
Lovells Cl. GU18: Ligh 6F 29
Lovel Rd. SL4: Wink 1E 11
Lowbury RG12: Brac 1E 17
Lwr. Broadmoor Rd.
RG45: Crow 4E 25
Lower Canes GU46: Yate 4E 33
Lwr. Church Rd.
GU47: Sand 1A 34
Lwr. Mill Fld. GU19: Bag 6B 28
Lower Moor GU46: Yate 5H 33
Lower Nursery SL5: S'dale . . .2C 20
Lwr. Sandhurst Rd.
RG40: Finch 6D 22
Lower Ter. RG41: Sind 4A 4
Lwr. Village Rd. SL5: S'hill . . .2F 19
Lwr. Wokingham Rd.
RG40: Finch 2H 23
RG45: Crow 2H 23
Lowlands Rd. GU17: Blac 6E 35
Lowry Cl. GU47: Coll T 4F 35
Lowther Cl. RG41: Woki 4D 4
Lowther Rd. RG41: Woki 3C 4
Lucas Cl. GU46: Yate 5H 33
Lucas Dr. GU46: Yate 5H 33
Luckley Path RG40: Woki 6G 5
(not continuous)
Luckley Rd. RG41: Woki 3F 13
Luckley Wood RG41: Woki . . .3F 13
Ludgrove RG40: Woki 3H 13
Ludlow RG12: Brac 4B 16
Lupin Ride RG45: Crow 6D 14
Lutterworth Cl. RG42: Brac . . .3C 8
Lychett Minster Cl.
RG12: Brac 2F 17
Lych Ga. Cl. GU47: Sand 2B 34
Lydbury RG12: Brac 6F 9
Lydney RG12: Brac 4B 16
Lymington Av. GU46: Yate . . .5F 33
Lyndhurst Av. GU17: Blac 4E 35
Lyndhurst Cl. RG12: Brac 6G 9
Lyndhurst Rd. SL5: Asc 1E 19
Lyneham Rd. RG45: Crow . . .3D 24
Lynwood Chase RG12: Brac . . .3C 8
Lynwood Cres. SL5: S'dale . . .3A 20
Lyon Oaks RG42: Warf 2B 8
Lyon Rd. RG45: Crow 2E 25
Lytham RG12: Brac 3G 15
Lytham Ct. SL5: S'hill 2G 19

M

Macadam Av. RG45: Crow . . .1E 25
Macbeth Ct. RG42: Warf 4E 9
McCarthy Way
RG40: Finch 6D 12
Machahon Cl. GU24: Chob . . .3G 31
McKernan Ct. GU47: Sand . . .2B 34
Maclaren Dr. RG42: Warf 4F 9
MACMILLAN HOUSE DAY
THERAPY UNIT (HOSPICE)
. . . . *1E 13*
(IN WOKINGHAM COMMUNITY
HOSPITAL)
Macphail Cl. RG40: Woki 4A 6
Macrae Rd. GU46: Yate 4G 33
Madingley RG12: Brac 5B 16
Madox Brown End
GU47: Coll T 3G 35
Madsar Gdns. RG40: Finch . . .2C 22
Magdalene Rd.
GU47: Owl 6H 25
Magnolia Cl. GU47: Owl 1F 35
RG42: Warf 4G 9
Magnolia Way
RG41: Woki 1D 12
Maidenhead Rd.
RG40: Woki 1A 6
RG42: Warf 1B 8
Maidensfield RG41: Winn 2B 4
Main Dr. RG42: Warf 3F 9
Mainprize Rd. RG12: Brac 4E 9
Maize La. RG42: Warf 2D 8
Makepiece Rd. RG42: Brac . . .3B 8
Malham Fell RG12: Brac 1A 16
Mallard Way GU46: Yate 4F 33
Mallowdale Rd.
RG12: Brac 4E 17
Malt Hill RG42: Warf 1E 9
Manor Cl. RG42: Brac 3A 8
Manor Ho. Dr. SL5: Asc 3E 11
Manor Pk. Dr. GU46: Yate . . .5H 33
RG40: Finch 2B 22
Manor Rd. RG41: Woki 4E 13
Manor Way GU19: Bag 6C 28
Mansfield Cl. SL5: Asc 4B 10
Mansfield Cres.
RG12: Brac 3B 16
Mansfield Pl. SL5: Asc 5B 10
Mansfield Rd.
RG41: Woki 1D 12
Manston Dr. RG12: Brac 3C 16
Maple Cl. GU17: Blac 5E 35
GU47: Sand 1B 34
RG41: Winn 1B 4
(off Meadow Vw.)
Maple Ct. RG12: Brac 1F 17
Maple Dr. RG45: Crow 1E 25
Maple Gdns. GU46: Yate 5H 33
Marbull Way RG42: Warf 2B 8
Marcheria Cl. RG12: Brac . . .3B 16
Marchmont Pl. RG12: Brac . . .6C 8
Mareshall Av. RG42: Warf 2B 8
Marigold Cl. RG45: Crow 1B 24
Market Pl. RG12: Brac 5B 8
RG40: Woki 6G 5
Market St. RG12: Brac 5B 8
Markham M. RG40: Woki 6F 5
Marks Rd. RG41: Woki 4E 5
Marlborough Ct.
RG40: Woki 5H 5
Mars Cl. RG41: Woki 6C 4
Marshall Rd. GU47: Coll T . . .3F 35
Marsham Ho. RG42: Brac 3B 8
Marsh La. RG27: Ever 3D 32
Marston Way SL5: Asc 5C 10
Martins Cl. GU17: Blac 6F 35
Martin's Dr. RG41: Woki 4F 5
MARTIN'S HERON **6F 9**
Martin's Heron Station (Rail)
. . . .**1F 17**
Martin's La. RG12: Brac 6E 9
Maryland RG40: Finch 6C 12
Mary Mead RG42: Warf 2D 8
Masefield Gdns.
RG45: Crow 5D 24
Mason Cl. GU46: Yate 5A 34
Mason Pl. GU47: Sand 2B 34
Matthews Chase
RG42: Binf 3H 7
Matthews Ct. SL5: S'hill 1H 19
MATTHEWSGREEN **4E 5**
Matthewsgreen Rd.
RG41: Woki 4E 5
Maxine Cl. GU47: Sand 1D 34
Maybrick Cl. GU47: Sand 1B 34
May Cl. GU47: Owl 2F 35
Mayfield Ct. RG27: Ever 2B 32
Mayflower Dr. GU46: Yate . . .3E 33
Mays Cft. RG12: Brac 1A 16
May's Rd. RG40: Woki 6A 6
Meachen Ct. RG40: Woki 6G 5
Meade Ct. GU19: Bag 5D 28
Meadow Cl. GU17: Haw 6F 35
Meadow Ho. GU17: Haw 6G 35
Meadow Rd. GU25: Vir W . . .2G 21
RG41: Woki 1E 13
Meadows, The
GU47: Coll T 5G 35
Meadows Bus. Pk., The
GU17: Blac 5G 35
Meadow Vw. RG41: Winn 1B 4
Meadow Wlk. RG41: Woki 6E 5
Meadow Way GU17: Blac 5E 35
RG41: Woki 1E 13
RG42: Brac 3A 8
Medhurst Cl. GU24: Chob . . .6H 31
MEDICAL RECEPTION STATION
(SANDHURST) **2H 35**
Medina Cl. RG41: Woki 5C 4
Medway Cl. RG41: Woki 5C 4
Melbourne Av. RG41: Winn . . .3A 4
Melksham Cl. GU47: Owl 1F 35
Melody Cl. RG41: Winn 1A 4
Melrose RG12: Brac 5B 16
Membury Wlk. RG12: Brac . . .1E 17
Mendip Rd. RG12: Brac 2E 17
Mercury Av. RG41: Woki 6C 4
Meridian Ct. SL5: Asc 5F 19
Merlewood RG12: Brac 2D 16
Merlin Clove RG42: Wink R . . .2H 9
Merron Cl. GU46: Yate 5G 33
Merrydene Ct. RG12: Binf 5E 7
MERRYHILL GREEN **1B 4**
Merryhill Grn. La.
RG41: Winn 1B 4
Merryhill Rd. RG42: Brac 3A 8
Merryman Dr. RG45: Crow . . .2B 24
Merryweather Cl.
RG40: Woki 5D 12
Merton Cl. GU47: Owl 6H 25
Metro Bus. Cen., The
RG41: Woki 2E 5
Michaelmas Cl.
GU46: Yate 6H 33
Micheldever Way
RG12: Brac 3F 17
Mickle Hill GU47: Sand 1C 34
Milbanke Ct. RG12: Brac 5H 7
Milbanke Way RG12: Brac 5H 7
Mileswood Farm Ind. Est.
RG40: Woki 5D 14
Millars Bus. Cen.
RG41: Woki 2E 13
Mill Bri. Rd. GU46: Yate 2F 33
Mill Cl. GU19: Bag 5B 28
RG41: Woki 5D 4
Millennium Way RG12: Brac . . .4B 8
Millers Thumb RG12: Brac 4E 9
Mill Fld. GU19: Bag 5B 28
Mill Grn. RG42: Binf 3G 7
Millins Cl. GU47: Owl 1G 35
Mill La. GU46: Yate 2H 33
RG12: Brac 1H 15
Mill Mead RG41: Woki 5E 5
Millmere GU46: Yate 3H 33
Mill Pond Rd. GU20: Wind . . .2F 29
Mill Ride SL5: Asc 4A 10
Milman Cl. RG12: Brac 5G 9
Milton Cl. RG12: Brac 3B 16
Milton Ct. RG40: Woki 5F 5
Milton Dr. RG40: Woki 5F 5
Milton Gdns. RG40: Woki 6F 5
Milton Rd. RG40: Woki 4F 5
Milward Gdns. RG12: Binf 5E 7
Minchin Grn. RG42: Binf 1E 7
Mincing La. GU24: Chob 5H 31
Minden Cl. RG41: Woki 6C 4
Minoru Pl. RG42: Binf 1F 7
Minstead Cl. RG12: Brac 6F 9
Minstead Dr. GU46: Yate 5G 33
Minster Ct. GU15: Camb 6H 35
Mistletoe Rd. GU46: Yate 6H 33
Mitre Pl. RG42: Warf 2B 8
Moffats Cl. GU47: Sand 2C 34
Moles Cl. RG40: Woki 1H 13
Molly Millars Bri.
RG41: Woki 2F 13
Molly Millars Cl.
RG41: Woki 2F 13
Molly Millar's La.
RG41: Woki 1E 13
Molyneux Rd. GU20: Wind 4H 29
Monks All. RG42: Binf 1D 6
Monks Cl. SL5: Asc 3F 19
Monks Dr. SL5: Asc 3F 19
Monkshood Cl. RG40: Woki . . .5A 6
Monks Wlk. SL5: Asc 3F 19
Mons Cl. RG41: Woki 6C 4
Montague Cl. RG40: Woki 4A 6
Monteagle La. GU46: Yate . . .5F 33
Montgomery Cl.
GU47: Sand 2D 34
Montgomery of Alamein Ct.
RG12: Brac 4D 8
Moor Cl. GU47: Owl 1G 35
RG40: Finch 1C 22
Moordale Av. RG42: Brac 4G 7
Moores Grn. RG40: Woki 4A 6
Moor La. RG12: Binf 6E 7
Moor Pk. Ho. *RG12: Brac 3G 15*
(off St Andrews)
Moor Pl. GU20: Wind 3F 29
Moors Ct. *RG40: Finch 6C 12*
(off Ditchfield La.)
Moray Av. GU47: Coll T 2F 35
(not continuous)
Mordaunt Dr. RG45: Crow . . .5D 24
Morden Cl. RG12: Brac 1F 17
Morley Cl. GU46: Yate 5F 33
Mornington Av.
RG40: Finch 6D 12
Mostyn Ho. *RG42: Brac 3B 8*
(off Merryhill Rd.)
Moulsham Copse La.
GU46: Yate 3F 33
Moulsham Grn.
GU46: Yate 3F 33
Moulsham La. GU46: Yate . . .3F 33
Mountbatten Ri.
GU47: Sand 1B 34
Mount La. RG12: Brac 6C 8
Mt. Pleasant GU47: Sand 1C 34
RG12: Brac 6C 8
RG41: Woki 6E 5

Mower Cl.—Plough Rd.

Mower Cl. RG40: Woki 5B 6
Muirfield Ho. *RG12: Brac 3G 15*
(off St Andrews)
Mulberry Bus. Pk. RG41: Woki 2E 13
Mulberry Cl. GU47: Owl 2F 35
RG45: Crow 4E 25
Mulberry Ct. RG12: Brac 2E 17
RG40: Woki 6G 5
Munday Ct. RG42: Binf 3G 7
Munnings Dr. GU47: Coll T 4F 35
Murdoch Rd. RG40: Woki 1G 13
Murray Ct. SL5: S'hill 3G 19
Murray Ho. RG41: Woki 6E 5
Murray Rd. RG41: Woki 6E 5
Murrell Hill La. RG42: Binf 3E 7
Mushroom Castle RG42: Wink R 2H 9
Mutton Hill RG12: Binf 4E 7
Mutton Oaks RG12: Binf 4F 7
Mylne Sq. RG40: Woki 6H 5
Myrtle Dr. GU17: Blac 5F 35

N

Napier Cl. RG45: Crow 3E 25
Napier Rd. RG45: Crow 4E 25
Napper Cl. SL5: Asc 5A 10
Naseby RG12: Brac 5B 16
Nash Gdns. SL5: Asc 5C 10
NASH GROVE 5C 12
Nashgrove La. RG40: Finch 4C 12
Nashgrove Ride RG41: Woki 4A 12
Nash Pk. RG42: Binf 2D 6
Nell Gwynne Av. SL5: S'hill 1H 19
Nell Gwynne Cl. SL5: S'hill 1H 19
Nelson Cl. RG12: Brac 4E 9
Nelson Way GU15: Camb 6H 35
Neptune Cl. RG41: Woki 6C 4
Netherton RG12: Brac 1A 16
Nettlecombe RG12: Brac 3D 16
Neuman Cres. RG12: Brac 3A 16
Nevelle Cl. RG42: Binf 4F 7
New Acres Mobile Home Pk. RG40: Woki 1A 24
Newark Rd. GU20: Wind 2F 29
NEWELL GREEN 1D 8
Newell Grn. RG42: Warf 1C 8
New Forest Ride RG12: Brac 1F 17
Newhurst Gdns. RG42: Warf 1D 8
Newlands Cl. GU46: Yate 5H 33
Newlands Farm Ind. Est. RG40: Woki 5D 14
Newmans Pl. SL5: S'dale 4D 20
New Mdw. SL5: Asc 4B 10
New Mile Rd. SL5: Asc 5F 11
Newport Dr. RG42: Warf 2B 8
New Rd. GU17: Haw 6G 35
GU19: Bag 5D 28
GU20: Bag, Wind 5D 28
GU47: Sand 2C 34
RG12: Brac 5D 8
RG27: Ever 3D 32
RG45: Crow 3E 25
SL5: Asc 3C 10
Newtown Rd. GU47: Sand 2D 34
New Wokingham Rd. RG40: Woki 1C 24
RG45: Crow 1C 24
Nightingale Cres. RG12: Brac 2C 16
Nightingale Gdns. GU47: Sand 2D 34
Nine Mile Ride RG12: Brac 6E 15
RG40: Finch 2A 22
SL5: Asc 4C 18
Nine Mile Ride Industry RG40: Finch 3A 22
Nook, The GU47: Sand 2C 34
Norfolk Chase RG42: Warf 3F 9
Norfolk Cl. RG41: Woki 6C 4
Norman Keep RG42: Warf 4F 9
Norreys Av. RG40: Woki 6H 5
Northampton Cl. RG12: Brac 6D 8
NORTH ASCOT 4B 10
Northbrook Copse RG12: Brac 3F 17
Northcott RG12: Brac 5A 16
North Dr. GU25: Vir W 3G 21
North End La. SL5: S'dale 4D 20
Northerams Woods Nature Reserve 1G 15
North Fryerne GU46: Yate 2H 33
North Grn. RG12: Brac 4D 8
Northington Cl. RG12: Brac 3F 17
Nth. Lodge Dr. SL5: Asc 5A 10
North Rd. SL5: Asc 4H 9
Northumberland Cl. RG42: Warf 3F 9
North Vw. RG12: Binf 6E 7
Northway RG41: Woki 5B 4
Norton Pk. SL5: S'hill 2G 19
Norton Rd. RG40: Woki 1G 13
Novello Theatre 2H 19
Nuffield Dr. GU47: Owl 1H 35
Nugee Ct. RG45: Crow 3D 24
Nuneaton RG12: Brac 3E 17
Nursery La. SL5: Asc 4C 10
Nuthurst RG12: Brac 2E 17
Nutley RG12: Brac 5A 16
Nutley Cl. GU46: Yate 5H 33

O

Oak Av. GU47: Owl 1F 35
Oakdale RG12: Brac 3D 16
Oakdene GU24: Chob 3H 31
SL5: S'dale 3B 20
Oakengates RG12: Brac 5A 16
Oakey Dr. RG40: Woki 1F 13
Oak Farm Cl. GU17: Blac 5E 35
Oakfield Ct. RG41: Woki 1D 12
Oakfield Rd. GU17: Haw 6G 35
OAK GROVE 4G 35
Oak Gro. Cres. GU15: Camb 4H 35
Oakhurst GU24: Chob 6G 31
Oaklands GU46: Yate 4H 33
Oaklands Bus. Cen. RG41: Woki 2E 13
(not continuous)
Oaklands Cl. SL5: Asc 3D 10
Oaklands Dr. RG41: Woki 2D 12
SL5: Asc 3D 10
Oaklands La. RG45: Crow 2C 24
Oaklands Pk. RG41: Woki 2E 13
Oak Leaf Ct. SL5: Asc 4B 10
Oak Lodge RG45: Crow 3E 25
Oakmede Pl. RG42: Binf 2E 7
Oaks, The GU46: Yate 5H 33
RG12: Brac 5D 8
Oak Tree M. RG12: Brac 6D 8
Oaktree Way GU47: Sand 1C 34
Oak Vw. RG40: Woki 2F 13
Oakwood Pl. RG45: Crow 4C 24
Oakwood Rd. GU20: Wind 4A 30
RG12: Brac 5E 9
Oareborough RG12: Brac 1E 17
Ocean Ho. RG12: Brac 5B 8
Octavia RG12: Brac 5A 16
Ogden Pk. RG12: Brac 6E 9
Okingham Cl. GU47: Owl 6F 25
Old Bakery M. RG42: Warf 1D 8
Old Bracknell Cl. RG12: Brac 6B 8
Old Bracknell La. E. RG12: Brac 6B 8
Old Bracknell La. W. RG12: Brac 6A 8
Oldbury RG12: Brac 6H 7
Oldcorne Hollow GU46: Yate 5E 33
Olde Farm Dr. GU17: Blac 4D 34
Old Farm Dr. RG42: Brac 3C 8
Old Forest Rd. RG41: Winn 4C 4
Old Forge End GU47: Sand 3D 34
Oldhouse La. GU20: Wind 5F 29
(not continuous)
Old Lands Hill RG12: Brac 4D 8
Old Monteagle La. GU46: Yate 4F 33
Old Pharmacy Ct. RG45: Crow 4D 24
Old Priory La. RG42: Warf 2D 8
Old Row Ct. RG40: Woki 6G 5
Old Sawmill La. RG45: Crow 2E 25
Old School La. GU46: Yate 4G 33
Oldstead RG12: Brac 2D 16
Old Welmore GU46: Yate 5A 34
Old Wokingham Rd. RG40: Woki 4D 14
RG45: Crow 6E 15
Old Woosehill La. RG41: Woki 5D 4
Oleander Cl. RG45: Crow 1B 24
Oliver Rd. SL5: Asc 1E 19
Olivia Ct. RG41: Woki 6F 5
Ollerton RG12: Brac 5A 16
Onslow Dr. SL5: Asc 3E 11
Onslow Rd. SL5: S'dale 4D 20
Opal Way RG41: Woki 5C 4
Opladen Way RG12: Brac 2C 16
Orbit Cl. RG40: Finch 2D 22
Orchard Cl. RG40: Woki 6H 5
Orchard Ct. RG12: Brac 5C 8
Orchard Ga. GU47: Sand 2D 34
Orchard Hill GU20: Wind 5H 29
Orchard Pl. RG40: Woki 6G 5
Oregon Wlk. RG40: Finch 1B 22
Oriental Rd. SL5: S'hill 1H 19
Orion RG12: Brac 5A 16
Ormathwaites Cnr. RG42: Warf 3E 9
Ormonde Rd. RG41: Woki 1E 13
Osborne La. RG42: Warf 1C 8
Osborne Rd. RG40: Woki 6G 5
Osman's Cl. RG42: Wink R 3H 9
Osterley Cl. RG40: Woki 1B 14
Oswald Cl. RG42: Warf 3E 9
Othello Gro. RG42: Warf 4E 9
Otter Cl. RG45: Crow 1C 24
Overbury Av. RG41: Woki 3D 4
Owen Rd. GU20: Wind 3H 29
Owl Cl. RG41: Woki 1C 12
OWLSMOOR 1G 35
Oxenhope RG12: Brac 1A 16
Oxford Rd. GU47: Owl 6G 25
RG41: Woki 5E 5
Oxfordshire Pl. RG42: Warf 3F 9

P

Paddock, The RG12: Brac 6C 8
RG45: Crow 2C 24
Page's Cft. RG40: Woki 1H 13
Paice Grn. RG40: Woki 5H 5
Pakenham Rd. RG12: Brac 4D 16
Palmer Cl. RG40: Woki 6C 14
Palmer Ct. RG40: Woki 6G 5
Palmer School Rd. RG40: Woki 6G 5
Pankhurst Dr. RG12: Brac 2D 16
Parade, The GU46: Yate 4A 34
Park Av. RG40: Woki 1F 13
(not continuous)
Park Cres. SL5: S'dale 3B 20
Park Dr. SL5: S'dale 3B 20
Parkers Ct. GU19: Bag 5C 28
Parkfield Ho. *RG45: Crow 4E 25*
(off Cambridge Rd.)
Parkfields GU46: Yate 5H 33
Parkhill Cl. GU17: Blac 6F 35
Parkhill Rd. GU17: Blac 6F 35
Parkland Dr. RG12: Brac 4E 9
Park La. RG40: Finch 3A 22
RG42: Binf 3G 7
Park Rd. GU47: Sand 3E 35
RG12: Brac 5D 8
RG40: Woki 6F 5
Parkside Rd. SL5: S'dale 3C 20
Park St. GU19: Bag 5C 28
Park Vw. GU19: Bag 5B 28
Parkway RG45: Crow 3C 24
Parsons Fld. GU47: Sand 2D 34
Parson's Ride RG12: Brac 4F 17
Parterre Pl. RG41: Winn 1A 4
Partridge Av. GU46: Yate 4F 33
Pathway, The RG42: Binf 1E 7
Patrick Gdns. RG42: Warf 3E 9
Patten Ash Dr. RG40: Woki 5A 6
Patten Av. GU46: Yate 5G 33
Paul's Fld. RG27: Ever 2B 32
Payley Dr. RG40: Woki 4A 6
Peach St. RG40: Woki 6G 5
Peacock Cotts. RG12: Brac 1E 15
Peacock La. RG12: Brac 2D 14
RG40: Woki 2D 14
Peacock Wlk. RG41: Woki 1C 12
Peddlars Gro. GU46: Yate 4A 34
Peel Cen., The RG12: Brac 5A 8
Peggotty Pl. GU47: Owl 6G 25
Pembroke RG12: Brac 4H 15
Pembroke Cl. SL5: S'hill 2H 19
Pembroke M. SL5: S'hill 2H 19
Pembroke Pde. GU46: Yate 3A 34
Pendine Pl. RG12: Brac 2B 16
Pendlebury RG12: Brac 4A 16
Peninsular Pl. RG45: Crow 4E 25
PENNYHILL PARK 6H 27
Pensford Cl. RG45: Crow 1D 24
Penwood Gdns. RG12: Brac 3F 15
Peregrine Cl. RG12: Brac 2B 16
RG41: Woki 1D 12
Perkins Way RG41: Woki 1E 13
Perryhill Dr. GU47: Sand 1B 34
Perry Oaks RG12: Brac 5E 9
Perry Way RG12: Brac 5E 9
Peterhouse Cl. GU47: Owl 6H 25
Petrel Cl. RG41: Woki 1C 12
Pewsey Va. RG12: Brac 2F 17
Pheasant Cl. RG41: Winn 2A 4
Phillip Copse RG12: Brac 4D 16
Phoenix Bus. Pk. RG12: Brac 5E 7
Phoenix Cl. RG41: Woki 6C 4
Pickering RG12: Brac 1A 16
Picket Post Cl. RG12: Brac 6F 9
Pigott Rd. RG40: Woki 4H 5
Pine Cl. GU15: Camb 3G 35
Pinecote Dr. SL5: S'dale 4B 20
Pine Ct. RG12: Brac 1E 17
Pine Cft. Rd. RG41: Woki 4E 13
Pine Dr. GU17: Haw 6G 35
RG40: Finch 1E 23
Pinefields Cl. RG45: Crow 3D 24
Pine Gro. GU20: Wind 4H 29
Pinehill Ri. GU47: Sand 2E 35
Pinehill Rd. RG45: Crow 4D 24
Pinehurst SL5: S'hill 2H 19
Pine Ridge Mobile Home Pk. RG40: Woki 1A 24
PINEWOOD 2D 24
Pinewood Av. RG45: Crow 2E 25
Pinewood Cvn. Pk. RG40: Woki 6E 15
Pinewood Cl. GU47: Sand 2B 34
Pinewood Gdns. GU19: Bag 5A 28
Pinewood Leisure Cen. 6D 14
Pinewood Rd. GU25: Vir W 1H 21
Pipson La. GU46: Yate 5H 33
Pipsons Cl. GU46: Yate 4H 33
Pitch Pl. RG42: Binf 1F 7
Pitts Cl. RG42: Binf 2F 7
Plantagenet Pk. RG42: Warf 4F 9
Plateau, The RG42: Warf 3G 9
Plaza, The RG40: Woki 1G 13
Ploughlands RG42: Brac 4H 7
Plough La. RG40: Woki 5B 6
Plough Rd. GU46: Yate 3A 34

44 A-Z Bracknell

T

The representation on the maps of a road, track or footpath is no evidence of the existence of a right of way.

The Grid on this map is the National Grid taken from Ordnance Survey® mapping with the permission of the Controller of Her Majesty's Stationery Office.

Copyright of Geographers' A-Z Map Company Ltd.